Useful Exercises
for
IELTS

International Edition

BY GARRY ADAMS &
TERRY PECK

ADAMS & AUSTEN PRESS - SYDNEY, AUSTRALIA

BY THE AUTHORS:

'101 Helpful Hints for IELTS - Academic Module'
International Edition - Practice Book & Cassette
> *Book:*   *ISBN # 0 9587604 6 2*
> *Cassette: ISBN # 0 9578980 0 2*

'101 Helpful Hints for IELTS - General Training Module'
International Edition - Practice Book & Cassette
> *Book:*   *ISBN # 0 9587604 9 7*
> *Cassette: ISBN # 0 9578980 0 2*

'202 Useful Exercises for IELTS'
International Edition - Practice Book & Cassette
> *Book:*   *ISBN # 0 9587604 7 0*
> *Cassette: ISBN # 0 9578980 1 0*

'202 Useful Exercises for IELTS'
Australasian Edition - Practice Book & Cassette
> *Book:*   *ISBN # 0 9587604 5 4*
> *Cassette: ISBN # 0 9578980 2 9*

AVAILABLE SOON:

'101 Helpful Hints for IELTS - Academic Module'
International Edition - Practice CD-ROM and Manual

'101 Helpful Hints for IELTS - General Training Module'
International Edition - Practice CD-ROM and Manual

'303 The Speaking Room for IELTS'
Video/CD-ROM/Cassette and Manual

'404 Practice Listening Tests for IELTS'
Practice Book & Cassettes
> *Book:*   *ISBN # 0 9587604 8 9*
> *Cassettes: ISBN # 0 9578980 4 5*

AUTHORS' ACKNOWLEDGEMENTS

We would like to acknowledge the support of the following people who assisted with the production of the cassette tape :

Bruce Bell, Richard Bird, Elena Carapetis, Sandra Eldridge, Ron Haddrick, Julie Hamilton, Salvatore Lista, Lorna Lesley, Nicola Martin, Helen Piotrowski, Paul Vaughan, and Peter Whitford.

ABOUT THE AUTHORS

Terry Peck and Garry Adams have extensive IELTS teaching experience, both being involved in the implementation and design of a number of IELTS coaching programmes. Terry Peck was an IELTS examiner for many years in Sydney, Australia.

First published in Sydney, Australia 2001
ISBN 0 9587604 7 0

Adams & Austen Press Pty. Ltd. A.B.N. 96 087 873 943
PO Box 509, Marrickville, New South Wales, Australia 1475
Tel/Fax: 612-9568-1768
Email: aap@aapress.com.au   www.aapress.com.au

Illustrations by H. Piotrowski and T. Peck

Printed and bound in Australia by Southwood Press, Marrickville, NSW.

9 8 7 6 5 4 3

CONTENTS

PREFACE

The 202 exercises contained in this practice workbook are designed to complement the information and practice tests contained in the authors' study books and guides to the IELTS examination, especially *'101 Helpful Hints for IELTS' (Academic Module* and *General Training Module* versions). However, it is not essential to refer to those books to complete the exercises.

All of the 202 exercises involve the various skills required to take the IELTS test, and most, but not all, of the questions asked in these exercises are of the type found in the actual test. For instance, questions that require grammatical knowledge are asked indirectly in the IELTS test itself, but are sometimes put to the student directly in this practice workbook (see the Grammar sections).

The book was written with 3 main purposes in mind. Carefully working through the 202 exercises should:

> ... provide varied practice to extend the skills referred to in the authors' study books and guides;

> ... highlight a student's probable weaknesses in 7 important areas of skill in English, - listening, reading, writing, punctuation, spelling, grammar and vocabulary;

> ... increase a student's general knowledge in 5 areas of current topical interest, namely, 'Communication and the Arts', 'The Environment', 'Technology', 'Politics in Britain', and 'Youth and Education'.

Also, speaking practice is included in this workbook to extend the value of certain exercises, but for a complete treatment refer to the authors' forthcoming production *'303 The Speaking Room'*.

May we take this opportunity to wish good luck to all students intending to take the IELTS examination soon.

January 2001

KEY TO ICONS

 Listening Exercises   Punctuation Exercises

 Reading Exercises   Spelling Exercises

 Writing Exercises   Grammar Exercises

 IELTS Quiz   Vocabulary Exercises

 Speaking Practice

LISTENING EXERCISES 1.1 - 1.9

1.1 SPEED LISTENING: Note only the essential details of what you hear: (Refer to the tapescript for confirmation.)

a. Edinburgh is ....

b. The city is ....

c. The annual ....

d. The centre ....

e. The New Town ....

f. The Old Town ....

g. The Festival ....

h. ....

i. ....

j. ....

1.2 NUMBERS AND LETTERS: (Refer to the tapescript for confirmation.)

A i. .... ii. .... iii. .... iv. .... v. ....

vi. .... vii. .... viii. .... ix. .... x. ....

B i. .... ii. .... iii. .... iv. ....

v. .... vi. .... vii. .... viii. ....

ix. .... x. ....

C i. .... ii. .... iii. .... iv. ....

v. .... vi. .... vii. .... viii. ....

ix. .... x. ....

D i. .... ii. .... iii. .... iv. .... v. ....

vi. .... vii. .... viii. .... ix. .... x. ....

1.3 GENERAL INFORMATION: Listen to Radio Items 1 & 2 and complete the chart with the basic details: (Refer to the tapescript for confirmation.)

	What?	Where?	When?	Who?	How?	Why?
Radio Item 1						
Radio Item 2						

1.4 GAPFILL: Listen to Radio Item 1 again and complete the gaps in the summary of the passage below with the correct word or phrase you hear:

Violent video (1)............... could be responsible for a rise in violence by children in society, but not enough (2)............... has been done to prove it. Although a disturbed child may (3)............... violently after playing a (4)............... computer game, it is possible that he or she will react similarly after a less violent stimulus. There is a great amount of violence on TV and in computer games because violence (5)............... well. Young (6)..............., however, play less violent games than young males, but this may be because of the way in which (7)............... companies package their products. Computer games are (8)............... ; unlike TV, playing games is not a passive activity. Perhaps children can relieve their (9)............... harmlessly in this way. Or maybe such games reward violence instead of punish it. If you agree, telephone (10)............... .

1.5 MULTIPLE CHOICE QUESTIONS: Listen to Radio Item 2 a second time and answer the following questions:

i. 'zines can be read:

a) on a word-processor
b) online
c) in a comic
d) none of the above

ii. Jean has published:

a) two issues of the 'zine
b) three issues
c) four issues
d) none of the above

iii. The 'zine called 'Fill Me In' is sold in:

a) supermarkets
b) alternative bookshops
c) second-hand bookshops
d) all of the above

iv. The publishing team's office is:

a) at home
b) in the Design College
c) in an alternative bookshop
d) in the front room of a bookshop

1.6 SPECIFIC INFORMATION: Listen again to the radio items:

RADIO ITEM 1

i. Who believes violent video games increase child violence?

ii. In the first section of the talk, violent video games are also described as being 'video games ____ _____ _____'.

iii. How are the video games that appeal to female players described?

iv. What may software companies be guilty of in the way they market games?

v. What are the onscreen rewards for violence in video games?

RADIO ITEM 2

i. Ordinary magazines fortunes 'ebb and flow'. What do you think this means?

ii. Jean's 'zine is described as 'another desk-topped magazine clone'. The word clone means a replica, or something modelled exactly on the original'. What is her 'zine a replica of?

iii. How many 'zines has Jean already sold?

iv. Where did Jean meet the other members of her publishing team?

v. What does Jean say is the reason for the success of her 'zine?

1.7 PREDICTION AND PREPARATION: In the Listening Sub-Test you are given very little time to look at the questions before the tape begins. However, you must use what time you are given wisely. Try to predict as much as you can about the content of a section you are about to hear, and circle key words and phrases that you should listen for.

Look at the questions in Exercises 1.8 and 1.9 and circle the keywords and phrases to listen for. Take no longer than 30 seconds.

Try to predict what you will hear on the tape. Ask yourself:

- who is probably talking and to whom?
- what is the precise topic that the person is likely to be talking about?

1.8 TRUE / FALSE / NOT GIVEN: Listen to Lecture 1 on the tape:

a.	No-one actually knows how one's first language is learnt.	T F NG
b.	There are very few facts known about how language is learnt.	T F NG
c.	Subliminal language learning can only take place overnight.	T F NG
d.	You do not need to listen closely to the words on the tape.	T F NG
e.	You learnt your first language quickly because you were exposed daily to new words.	T F NG
f.	Watching TV or playing the radio in a foreign language is useless.	T F NG
g.	The words on the subliminal tape must be spoken softly and slowly.	T F NG
h.	You should restrict the number of new words when starting to learn a language.	T F NG
i.	Reading a foreign newspaper is never a waste of time.	T F NG
j.	The author thinks that learning a new language in six weeks is possible.	T F NG

1.9 SHORT-ANSWER QUESTIONS: Refer to Lecture 1 on the tape.

Note that the answers below have a *MAXIMUM NUMBER OF FOUR WORDS*:

i. Who have many theories to explain language learning?

....

ii. Name two suggested times for playing subliminal learning tapes:

1. ....

2. ....

iii. What do babies react to in the mother's womb?

....

iv. A vocabulary of how many words is required to learn basic English?

....

v. What important difference is there between people who speak other languages?

....

(ANSWERS ON PAGE 111)

▰ READING EXERCISES 1.1 - 1.11

☺ **1.1 PREDICTION:** Look at the illustration below and the words and phrases taken from the Reading Passage on the next page. With a partner if possible, try to predict exactly what is being discussed:

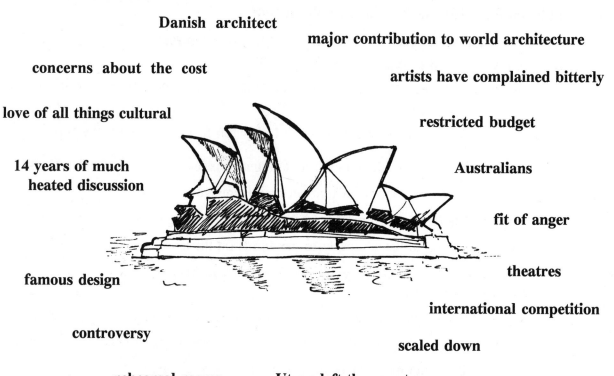

Danish architect

major contribution to world architecture

concerns about the cost

artists have complained bitterly

love of all things cultural

restricted budget

14 years of much heated discussion

Australians

fit of anger

famous design

theatres

international competition

controversy

scaled down

rehearsal rooms   Utzon left the country

☺ **1.2 PRE-READING QUESTIONS:** Before reading the text on the following page, work with a partner and ask and answer the questions below. Base your answers on your possible knowledge of the topic:

❏ Can you name at least 6 different forms of art that make up what is known as 'the arts'?

❏ What role do you think the arts play in a modern society?

❏ What art forms are popular in your country and culture? (painting? sculpture?) Why?

❏ Where are the performing arts performed in your city? Have you seen any shows there?

❏ Do you know who officially opened the Sydney Opera House in 1975?

❏ How much did the Opera House cost to build? £5 million? £15 million? £50 million?

Next, reorder the words in the mystery questions below:

1. **describe How House you Sydney the the of would shape Opera ?**
....

2. **the chosen when design was House the and of Opera How ?**
....

1.3 SKIMMING: Read the text once for the gist (overall idea) and then in detail:

══

1   It is almost impossible to write of the Arts in Australia without mentioning the building that first put the country firmly on the world cultural map - the Sydney Opera House. Completed in 1973 after 14 years of much heated discussion and at a cost of almost £60 million, it is not only the most well-known Australian building in the world but perhaps
5   the most famous design of any modern building anywhere.

    Its distinctive and highly original shape has been likened to everything from the sails of a sailing ship to broken eggshells, but few would argue with the claim that the Opera House is a major contribution to world architecture. Set amidst the graceful splendour of Sydney Harbour, presiding like a queen over the bustle and brashness of a modern city
10   striving to forge a financial reputation in a tough commercial world, it is a reminder to all Australians of their deep and abiding love of all things cultural.

    The Opera House was designed not by an Australian but by a celebrated Danish architect, Jorn Utzon, whose design won an international competition in the late 1950s. However, it was not, in fact, completed to his original specifications. Plans for much of the intended
15   interior design of the building have only recently been discovered. Sadly, the State Government of the day interfered with Utzon's plans because of concerns about the escalating cost, though this was hardly surprising - the building was originally expected to cost only £5.5 million. Utzon left the country before completing the project and in a fit of anger vowed never to return. The project was eventually paid for by a State-run lottery.

20   The size of the interior of the building was scaled down appreciably by a team of architects whose job it was to finish construction within a restricted budget. Rehearsal rooms and other facilities for the various theatres within the complex were either made considerably smaller or cut out altogether, and some artists have complained bitterly about them ever since. But despite the controversy that surrounded its birth, the Opera House has risen
25   above the petty squabbling and is now rightfully hailed as a modern architectural masterpiece. The Queen officially opened the building in 1975 and since then, within its curved and twisted walls, audiences of all nationalities have been quick to acclaim the many world-class performances of stars from the Australian opera, ballet and theatre.

══

1.4 WORD DEFINITIONS: Find the single words in paragraphs 1 and 2 which mean the following:

i.	pleasing, attractive	....	v.	characteristic	....
ii.	angry	....	vi.	(to) advance steadily	....
iii.	excited activity	....	vii.	trying hard	....
iv.	permanent, lasting	....	viii.	rashness	....

Next, find the words in paragraphs 3 and 4 which mean the following:

i.	meant	....	vi.	considerably	....
ii.	meddled with	....	vii.	(to) promise	....
iii.	made smaller	....	viii.	unimportant	....
iv.	limited	....	ix.	(to) applaud loudly	....
v.	known as	....	x.	money plan	....

1.5 TEXT ANALYSIS:

i. Which is the best title for the passage in Exercise 1.3?

a) Utzon Quits Australia

c) History of a Queen

b) An Architectural Disaster

d) A Dane in Our Lives

ii. What is the main point of the second paragraph?

a) ... to describe the
    Opera House visually

c) ... to state where
    the Opera House is located

b) ... to tell the
    history of the building

d) ... to say why
    the building was built

iii. Which is (are) the topic sentence(s) of the third paragraph?

a) Sentence number one

c) The last sentence

b) Sentence number two

d) Sentences number one and two

iv. To what do the following pronouns in the passage refer?

a) it   *(line 10)*   ....

c) this   *(line 17)*   ....

b) their   *(line 11)*   ....

d) them   *(line 23)*   ....

1.6 GAPFILL: The following is a summary of the passage in Exercise 1.3. Choose words from the box below and refer to the passage to fill the gaps:

The Sydney Opera House is one of the most famous (1)............... buildings in the world. Officially opened in (2)............... , its eye-catching and (3)............... shape was the dream of a Danish (4)............... called Utzon. Unfortunately, his design for the (5)............... could not be completed for financial reasons. Nonetheless, the building was finally ready after (6)............... years of (7)............... and argument, and is now (8)............... as a (9)............... of modern architecture. World-class performances are regularly given in the Opera House by Australian (10)............... from the worlds of opera, ballet and theatre.

architecture	1973	famous	queen	controversy	£5.5 million
interior	artists	modern	hail	acclaimed	exterior
originally	14	petty	architect	1975	rehearsals
masterpiece	distinctive	star	curve	£60 million	the 1950s

1.7 WORDS & PHRASES WITH SIMILAR MEANINGS: Refer to the passage in Exercise 1.3, and see page 126 for advice on recognising pattern types. Circle the appropriate pattern type in each case.

i.   well-known design   → *(para. 1)* .... (Pattern Type: **1   2   3**)

ii. angry talk   → *(para. 1)* .... (Pattern Type: **1   2   3**)

iii. located amidst   → *(para. 2)* .... (Pattern Type: **1   2   3**)

iv. competitive world   → *(para. 2)* .... (Pattern Type: **1 2 3**)

v. original designs   → *(para. 3)* .... (Pattern Type: **1 2 3**)

vi. restricted budget   → *(para. 4)* .... (Pattern Type: **1 2 3**)

vii. petty quarrelling   → *(para. 4)* .... (Pattern Type: **1 2 3**)

1.8 MATCHING SENTENCE HALVES: Refer to the text in Exercise 1.3 and match the halves of the given sentences together:

a. The Sydney Opera House ...   + ...

b. The city of Sydney is ...   + ...

c. Plans for the interior of the building ...   + ...

d. The interior of the building was unfortunately never ...   + ...

e. It seems that some artists are only ...   + ...

f. The cost of the project ...   + ...

g. ... interesting to audiences from all over the world.

h. ... have recently been implemented.

i. ... built like a queen on Sydney Harbour.

j. ... completed by Jorn Utzon.

k. ... was the most well-known building in Australia.

l. ... was not completed in accordance with the architect's original plans.

m. ... described as trying hard to survive in the business world.

n. ... were lost for many years.

o. ... interested in complaining about the facilities.

p. ... was eventually met from the proceeds of gambling.

1.9 TRUE / FALSE / NOT GIVEN: Refer to the text in Exercise 1.3.

a. The building is possibly the most famous of its type in the world.   **T F NG**

b. The Opera House drew world attention to the Arts in Australia.   **T F NG**

c. Utzon designed the roof to look like the sails of a sailing ship.   **T F NG**

d. A few people claim that it is a major architectural work.   **T F NG**

e. According to the author, Sydney is a quiet and graceful city.   **T F NG**

f. The cost of construction went more than £50 million over budget.   **T F NG**

g. Utzon never returned to Australia to see the completed building.   **T F NG**

h. There is only one theatre within the complex.   **T F NG**

i. The Government was concerned about some artists' complaints.   **T F NG**

j. Australian artists give better performances in the Opera House.   **T F NG**

1.10 SHORT-ANSWER QUESTIONS: Refer to the text in Exercise 1.3.

i. What two images have the shape of the Opera House roof been compared to:

1. ....

2. ....

ii. Why is it almost impossible to talk of the Arts in Australia without mentioning the Opera House?

....

iii. What did the government hold to ensure a world-class design for the building? *(MAXIMUM OF TWO WORDS)*

....

iv. What does the author say is not surprising?

....

v. What were cut out or scaled down from the original interior design?

....

vi. How are the walls of the Opera House described? *(MAXIMUM OF TWO WORDS)*

....

1.11 CROSSWORD: Refer to the Part 1 Listening Passages and the Reading Passage (and questions) for most answers.

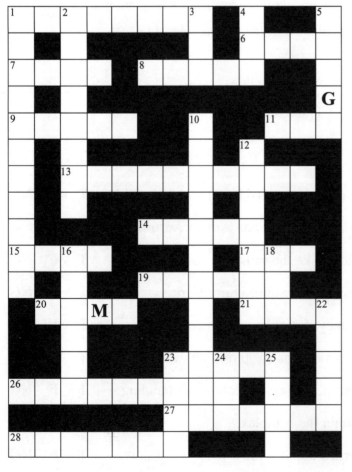

Across:
1. related to the Arts or the mind (adj)
6. region (n)
7. not any (adj)
8. unimportant, small (adj)
9. circular (adj)
11. present plural form of 'to be' (n)
13. not trusting of something (adj)
14. (to) apply colours to a drawing (v)
15. an important person in the arts (n)
17. (to) flow back like the tide (v)
19. opposite of 'practice' (n)
20. shown on your watch (n)
21. period of time (n)
23. many (adj)
26. (to) meddle (v)
27. lessened (adj)
28. dramatic performance artform (n)

Down:
1. dispute often about a topical issue (n)
2. person who studies languages (n)
3. (to) allow (v)
4. (to) tell (v)
5. region between certain limits (n)
10. science of building structures (n)
12. gambling with numbered tickets (n)
16. among (prep)
18. short for 'goodbye' (n)
22. quick (adj)
23. only, no more nor better than (adj)
24. past form of 'lead' (v)
25. length measurement (n)

(ANSWERS ON PAGE 111)

✍ WRITING EXERCISES 1.1 - 1.7

1.1 SENTENCE INSERTION: Practice for Writing Task 1:

First, insert the statistical information from the table below in the twenty numbered blank spaces in the model answer and in the 'missing' sentences labelled 'a' to 'e'. Then insert the missing sentences into the model answer.

The table below summarises some data collected by a college bookshop for the month of February 2000.

Write a report describing the sales figures of various types of publications, based on the information shown in the table.

	Non– Book Club Members			*Book Club Members*	Total
	College Staff	College Students	Members of Public		
Fiction	44	31	-	76	151
Non-Fiction	29	194	122	942	1287
Magazines	332	1249	82	33	1696
Total	405	1474	204	1051	3134

WRITING TASK 1 - Model Answer:

para.1 The table shows the sales figures of fiction books, non-fiction books, and magazines in a college bookshop for February (1)_____ . **(i)**... .

para.2 The non– Book Club member figures comprise sales to college staff, college students, and members of the public. **(ii)**... . College students bought (2)_____ magazines, (3)_____ non-fiction and (4)_____ fiction books. **(iii)**... . Although no fiction books were sold to members of the public, they purchased (5)_____ non-fiction books and (6)_____ magazines.

para.3 **(iv)**... . On the other hand, magazine sales to Club members ((7)_____) were fewer than for any other type of customer.

para.4 The total number of publications sold for the month was (8)_____ ((9)_____ to college students, (10)_____ to staff, (11)_____ to the public, and (12)_____ to Book Club members). **(v)**... . Therefore, magazines accounted for the greatest number of sales ((13)_____).

a.	College staff bought (14)_____ magazines, (15)_____ fiction and (16)_____ non-fiction books.
b.	More magazines were sold to college students than to any other group of customers.
c.	The figures are divided into two groups: sales to non– Book Club members and to Book Club members.
d.	Of this figure, (17)_____ items were fiction books and (18)_____ were non-fiction.
e.	Book Club members bought more fiction ((19)_____) and non-fiction books ((20)_____) than other customers.

1.2 PASSIVE CONSTRUCTION PRACTICE: Writing Task 1:

Identify the number of instances of the passive voice in the completed model answer on the previous page. Some are in the present and some are in the past. Can you explain why?

Next, rewrite the sentences below with the **underlined** verbs in the **passive**:

a.   The data in the graph <u>give</u> figures for both males and females.

   ....

b.   The table <u>shows</u> information regarding TV sales to various age-groups.

   ....

c.   The statistics displayed by the bar chart <u>include</u> data on radio listeners.

   ....

d.   The chart <u>denotes</u> figures for the rate of vocabulary acquisition at various ages.

   ....

e.   The diagram <u>divides</u> into four sections, one for each language.

   ....

f.   The user <u>places</u> the CD into the CD-ROM and the program <u>loads</u> into memory.

   ....

g.   The music store <u>sold</u> 2000 CDs in the month of May to persons aged 20-25.

   ....

1.3 THE TOPIC & THE TOPIC QUESTION: Writing Task 2:

Circle the topic and write the topic question as a 'wh' or yes/no question:

Example: (*'Studying the English language in an English-speaking country*) *is the best but not the only way to learn the language.'*

(It) is the best.. but is it the only way to learn a language? ....

a.   Compare the success of various methods of learning a foreign language. Give advice to students intending to learn another language.

   ....

b.   To what extent does television have a negative effect on society? Discuss the effect of widespread television viewing.

   ....

c.   The Arts should be better funded by the government, but there must be more control over where the money goes. Discuss.

   ....

1.4 LINKING AND SEQUENCING WORDS: Writing Task 2:

Your college tutor has asked you to write a short essay on the following topic:

'Studying the English language in an English-speaking country is the best but not the only way to learn the language.'

WRITING TASK 2 - Model Answer: Add linking and sequencing words from the box below:

para.1 Studying a language in a country where it is widely spoken has many advantages. It is (1)_____ a good idea to study English in a country such as Britain. (2)_____ , I believe it is not the only way to learn the language.

para.2 (3)_____ , most students in non–English-speaking countries learn English at secondary school and sometimes at university nowadays. (4)_____ their spoken English is not usually of very high standard, their knowledge of grammar is often quite advanced. This is certainly useful when students come to an English-speaking country to perfect the language.

para.3 (5)_____ , studying the basics of English at secondary school is less stressful than learning the language while overseas. This is because students living at home do not have to worry about problems such as finding accommodation, paying for their study and living costs, and trying to survive in a foreign country where day to day living causes much stress.

para.4 (6)_____ , there are obvious advantages of learning English in Britain. Every day there are opportunities to practise listening to and speaking with British people. (7)_____ , students can experience the culture first-hand, which is a great help when trying to understand the language. This is especially true if they choose to live with a British family, as exchange students for example. (8)_____ , if students attend a language school full-time, the teachers will be native speakers. In this case, (9)_____ will students speaking and listening skills improve, (10)_____ attention can be given to developing reading and writing skills as well.

para.5 (11)_____ , (12)_____ it is preferable to study English in an English-speaking country, a reasonable level of English can be achieved in one's own country, if a student is gifted and dedicated to study.

therefore	....	**however** (x2)	....	**although**	....
in general	....	**also**	....	**furthermore**	....
secondly	....	**even though**	....	**but**	....
in the first place	....	**not only**	....		

1.5 ARTICLES: Next, cover the model answer above and add the missing articles where necessary to the following sentences taken from the answer:

a. Studying (1)_____ language in (2)_____ country where it is widely spoken has many (3)_____ advantages. It is therefore (4)_____ good idea to study (5)_____ English in (6)_____ country such as (7)_____ Britain. However, I believe it is not (8)_____ only way to learn (9)_____ language.

b. Secondly, (10)_____ studying (11)_____ basics of (12)_____ English at (13)_____ secondary school is less stressful than learning (14)_____ language while overseas.

c. Every day there are (15)_____ opportunities to practise (16)_____ listening to and (17)_____ speaking with (18)_____ British people. Also, (19)_____ students can experience (20)_____ culture first-hand, which is (21)_____ great help when trying to understand (22)_____ language.

d. In general, even though it is preferable to study (23)_____ English in (24)_____ English-speaking (25)_____ country, (26)_____ reasonable level of (27)_____ English can be achieved in (28)_____ one's own country, if (29)_____ student is gifted and dedicated to (30)_____ study.

1.6 SCRAMBLED SENTENCES: Without looking at Exercise 1.4, unscramble the following sentences taken from the model answer:

a. of learning │ English │ there are │ in Britain │ obvious advantages

   ....

b. to understand │ when trying │ a great help │ which is │ the culture first-hand │ can experience │ the language │ students

   ....

c. native speakers │ if │ will be │ attend │ the teachers │ full-time │ students │ a language school

   ....

d. English │ to │ English-speaking │ an │ study │ country │ in │ it │ preferable │ is

   ....

e. of │ reasonable level │ gifted and dedicated │ can be achieved │ study │ to │ one's own country │ English │ is │ a │ a │ in │ student │ if

   ....

1.7 PREPOSITIONS AND PUNCTUATION: Add the missing prepositions and punctuate these sentences from the passage in Exercise 1.4:

a. although their spoken english is not usually (1)___ a very high standard their knowledge (2)___ grammar is often quite advanced

b. students living (3)___ home do not have (4)___ worry (5)___ problems such as finding accommodation paying (6)___ their study and living costs and trying (7)___ survive (8)___ a foreign country where day to day living causes much stress

c. there are obvious advantages (9)___ learning english (10)___ britain every day there are opportunities (11)___ practise listening (12)___ and speaking (13)___ native speakers

d. this is especially true if they choose (14)___ live (15)___ a british family as exchange students (16)___ example

(ANSWERS ON PAGE 112)

✿ SPELLING RULES 1.1 - 1.4

In each of the exercises below match the example to the rule. Note that there are exceptions to the rules - marked with an asterisk (*). These are given with the answers:

1.1 RULES FOR ADDING SUFFIXES:

    a.   **enlarge - enlargement / mere - merely**   →   example of RULE ......

    b.   **fine + er = finer / fit + ed = fitted**   →   example of RULE ......

    c.   **free, freeing, freed**   →   example of RULE ......

Rule 1. *Words ending with a consonant followed by an 'e': drop the 'e' before a suffix beginning with a vowel. (* see also Rules 10 & 11.)*

Rule 2. *Suffixes beginning with a consonant: keep the final 'e'. (*)*

Rule 3. *Words ending in 'ee': do not drop the 'e' before a suffix.*

1.2 RULES FOR DOUBLING CONSONANTS:

    a.   **travel - travelling / dial - dialling**   →   example of RULE ......

    b.   **big + er = bigger**   →   example of RULE ......

    c.   **in<u>fer</u> + ed = inferred / <u>o</u>m<u>it</u> + ed = omitted**   →   example of RULE ......

Rule 4. *Words with 1 syllable and 1 vowel which end in a single consonant: double the consonant before a suffix beginning with a vowel.*

Rule 5. *Words with 2 or 3-syllables ending with a single vowel followed by a single consonant: if the stress is on the last syllable, double the final consonant.*

Rule 6. *Words ending in 'l' after a single vowel (or two separately pronounced vowels): double the 'l'.*

1.3 RULES WITH 'Y' AND 'I':

    a.   **marry + ed = married / busy + er = busier**   →   example of RULE ......

    b.   **ceiling / conceit / believe / chief**   →   example of RULE ......

    c.   **convey + ed = conveyed / play + er = player**   →   example of RULE ......

Rule 7. *Words ending in 'y' after a consonant: change the 'y' to 'i' before a suffix except 'ing'.*

Rule 8. *When a 'y' comes after a vowel: do not change the vowel. (*)*

Rule 9. *The vowel 'i' comes before 'e' except after 'c'. (*)*

1.4 RULES FOR WORDS ENDING IN 'FUL', 'CE' AND 'GE':

    a.   **colour + full = colourful**   →   example of RULE ......

    b.   **skill + full = skilful**   →   example of RULE ......

    c.   **space - spacious**   →   example of RULE ......

    d.   **enforce - enforceable / courage - courageous**   →   example of RULE ......

Rule 10. *Words ending in 'ce' or 'ge': keep the 'e' before suffixes beginning with 'a', 'o' or 'u'.*

Rule 11. *Words ending in 'ce': change the 'e' to 'i' before 'ous'.*

Rule 12. *When adding 'ful' to a word: drop the second 'l'. (*)*

Rule 13. *When adding 'ful' to a word ending in 'll': drop the second 'l'.*

(ANSWERS ON PAGE 113)

✳ GRAMMAR EXERCISES 1.1 - 1.4

1.1 PARTS OF SPEECH: Decide on the part of speech for each of the words in **bold** in the following short passage:

1   It is exceedingly **difficult** to ascertain **precisely** what is meant by the **word** 'culture'. The word is commonly used to refer to **almost** anything connected **with** a person's **customary** behaviour when **considered** distinctive in form to **that** of a person from another **background**. The problem is that this definition begs **the** question. Is
5   it race that **determines** the difference in culture? Or is **it** nationhood? Certainly, there are noticeable cultural differences between citizens of **various** nations, **although** they may share **membership** of the same race. Is language **perhaps** the determinant of culture? Or class? After all, **even** within the same nation there are **extreme** differences **between** the lifestyle **and** language of the classes that **make up** a society, as well as
10   varying attitudes towards **acceptable** behaviour and manners. The problem appears to be that, on **closer** analysis, each and every one of **us** belongs to **a** unique culture, regardless of the **apparent** general culture into which **we** are categorised. It all depends on how narrowly the word is defined for **its** intended purpose. By **analysing** the word 'culture', anthropologists are **beginning** to accept that the word is much overworked.

line 1	1. difficult	
	2. precisely	
	3. word	
line 2	4. almost	
	5. with	
line 3	6. customary	
	7. considered	
	8. that	
line 4	9. background	
	10. the	
line 5	11. determines	
	12. it	
line 6	13. various	
	14. although	
line 7	15. membership	
	16. perhaps	
line 8	17. even	
	18. extreme	
line 9	19. between	
	20. and	
	21. make up	
line 10	22. acceptable	
line 11	23. closer	
	24. us	
	25. a	
line 12	26. apparent	
	27. we	
line 13	28. its	
	29. analysing	
line 14	30. beginning	

Choose between the following grammatical categories or parts of speech:

noun
pronoun
- possessive pronoun
gerund
adjective
verb
- past participle
- present participle
phrasal verb
adverb
preposition
conjunction
definite article
indefinite article

1.2 UNFINISHED SENTENCES?:
Underline the **nouns** (or **noun phrases**) in the following part or whole sentences. Next, circle the **verbs**. Then, complete the sentences with either a **full-stop** if the sentence is already complete, or with **suitable words** of your own choice.

a. Television, a recent invention, has changed the way in which we view the world

b. The photographer who had the best photograph in the competition

c. Few people know that the world's first feature film was made in Australia

d. The film medium, which is an extremely difficult art form to learn, I think

e. When studying a foreign language, students should follow a regular study plan

f. Watching movies in English, a good way to increase your listening skills

g. If you are earnest about improving your writing

h. The essay, Writing Task 2, is perhaps the most difficult of all the IELTS test tasks

i. Pronunciation of the language you are learning, always difficult for students

j. These days you can find opportunities to practise your English almost everywhere in Europe

k. One of the most remarkable sculptures in the world of art, Michelangelo's 'David'

l. Although ballet is seldom appreciated, which is a pity

m. One way of emphasizing what one says in a conversation, if the intent is to strongly suggest that what is being said is the truth, is to use open hand gestures

n. Evaluation of an argument in an essay can only be successful when the rules of formal essay writing, committed to memory

1.3 SUBJECT AND VERB AGREEMENT:
Check and correct the subject and verb agreement where necessary in the following sentences:

a. The pen and the paper is on the desk.

b. The box of chocolates are on the shelf.

c. Every one of the students have practised very hard.

d. The skill of understanding personal communications is crucial to good business.

e. Not many people know the truth about the lifestyles of the rich and famous.

f. The number of people who are mobile phone owners rise every year.

g. It used to be thought that learning languages waste time.

h. A great many success stories are due to hard work.

i. She is taking the test twice because she believe it is best to have a trial run.

j. In the '50s, the comedy team of Abbott and Costello were world famous.

k. Every day there is another driver who lose his driving licence due to speed.

l. None of the students sit at the back of the lecture theatre.

m. No-one know exactly why economics are more important now than in the past.

n. Neither of the debates were successful.

1.4 TENSES: Choose the correct words or phrases that are missing in the following sentences, paying attention to the correct tense required:

i.   Nobody believes that investment in telecommunications .... lose money.
  a) has ever   c) would ever
  b) had ever   d) will ever

ii. After .... her lunch, the teacher began marking the essays.
  a) finished   c) finishing
  b) had finished   d) having finish

iii. The student .... very well in her first practical examination.
  a) did   c) had done
  b) has done   d) all of the above

iv. It is hard to know why undergraduates .... help with their assignments.
  a) fail to seek   c) are not seeking
  b) will not seek   d) all of the above

v.   Most of the general public .... to see a live theatrical performance.
  a) have ever been c) are never wanting
  b) have never been d) all of the above

vi. Sometimes it is necessary to be careful .... the right date to sit for a test.
  a) when choosing   c) when you have choose
  b) when you will choose d) when you chose

vii. No-one who .... visited the Sydney Opera House is likely to forget it.
  a) will have   c) had ever
  b) would have   d) has ever

viii. If only the Prime Minister .... his arts policy would lose him the election.
  a) knows   c) was knowing
  b) had known   d) could have knowing

ix. If writing skills .... so important, why do candidates not practise more regularly?
  a) were   c) are
  b) would be   d) all of the above

x.   The better universities .... free classes to students with language problems.
  a) offering   c) should have offer
  b) is offering   d) offer

xi. The student .... studying at an institution when he had to return to his home country unexpectedly.
  a) is considering c) should consider
  b) was considering d) has considered

xii. The businesswoman .... dismissed because of her lack of politeness.
  a) could be   c) will be
  b) could have been d) all of the above

(ANSWERS ON PAGE 113)

★ VOCABULARY EXERCISES 1.1 - 1.3

1.1 SUFFIXES (1): Note the meanings of the 4 suffixes given in the box below. Then work out the approximate meaning of the words that follow before checking their meanings in a good dictionary:

ful = with	**able** = can be, able to be, must be,
less = without	**en** = make

artful ....

masterful ....

hapless ....

cashless society ....

justifiable ....

notifiable ....

hearten ....

enlighten ....

1.2 SUFFIXES (2): Can you think of three more words ending with each of the suffixes listed in the exercise above?

1.3 WORD FORMATION: Complete the chart to provide the correct form of the words shown for the given parts of speech: (Not all forms are possible.)

NOUNS			ADJECTIVE	VERB	ADVERB
PLACE *	**PERSON**	**GERUND/THING**			
-				write	-
-		designing/design			
	artist			-	
-			communicative		
-	-	expression			
-	-			mean	
	informant				
-	-		explanatory		-
-	-			conclude	
development					-
-	-				encouragingly

* double word nouns are possible

(ANSWERS ON PAGE 113)

LISTENING EXERCISES 2.1 - 2.9

2.1 SPEED LISTENING: Note only the essential details of what you hear: (Refer to the tapescript for confirmation.)

a. Cardiff has ....

b. This city ....

c. Wales ....

d. More than ....

e. Nuclear ....

f. The major ....

g. Cardiff ....

h. ....

i. ....

j. ....

2.2 NUMBERS AND LETTERS: (Refer to the tapescript for confirmation.)

A i. .... ii. .... iii. .... iv. .... v. ....

vi. .... vii. .... viii. .... ix. .... x. ....

B i. - x. ....

....

....

C i. .... ii. .... iii. .... iv. ....

v. .... vi. .... vii. .... viii. ....

ix. .... x. ....

D i. .... ii. .... iii. .... iv. .... v. ....

vi. .... vii. .... viii. .... ix. .... x. ....

2.3 GENERAL INFORMATION: Listen to Radio Items 3 & 4 and complete the chart with the basic details: (Refer to the tapescript for confirmation.)

	What?	Where?	When?	Who?	How?	Why?
Radio Item 3						
Radio Item 4						

2.4 GAPFILL: Listen to Radio Item 3 again and complete the gaps in the summary of the passage below with the correct word or phrase you hear:

The Earth's surface is two-thirds water, yet most of this is undrinkable or unusable because it is either seawater or (1)................ .   Of the 1% that is available as (2).............. water, most is used for (3).............. or goes to industry. Freshwater contamination is the major problem since it is all too easy to pollute rivers and streams with pesticides, industrial waste, and (4)................ .   In poor and (5).............. countries, the addition of sewage to sources of water leads to (6).............. and death. In China, a United Nations report estimates that over 78% of people drink from (7).............. water supplies. Although humankind has made enormous efforts to control the supply of fresh water by constructing more than (8)............... dams throughout the world, falling water (9)..............., shrinking rivers and lakes, and loss of wildlife are the result. School project kits are available by telephoning this number: (10).................. .

2.5 MULTIPLE CHOICE QUESTIONS: Listen to Radio Item 4 one more time and answer the following questions:

i. Residents believed the explosions were:

    a) caused by gas

    b) caused by storms

    c) planes nose-diving into the sea

    d) all of the above

ii. Professor Blunt was asked to help by:

    a) the University of Queensland

    b) the Shire Council

    c) the Biology Department

    d) the Port Charles resort

iii. The problem's solution involves:

    a) blasting the jellyfish out of the sea

    b) trapping jellyfish in the rock shelf

    c) changing the patterns of the tides

    d) none of the above

iv. More than half the rock shelf:

    a) will remain

    b) will be blasted away

    c) is the result of global warming

    d) is protected by environmentalists

2.6 SPECIFIC INFORMATION: Listen again to the radio items:

RADIO ITEM 3

i.   What is the name of the environmental radio programme?

ii. What are you told about the distribution pattern of fresh water in the world?

iii. What percentage of fresh water is available for personal use?

iv. What do rivers and streams feed that supply us with fresh water?

v.   Why are trees, plants and wildlife at risk?

RADIO ITEM 4

i.   Where did the explosions take place?

ii. What does the town rely on for its survival? (oil rigs? fishing? etc.)

iii. What can you no longer do in the waters off Carrsville?

iv. What is Professor Blunt's solution to the problem?

v.   For what is global warming thought to be partly responsible?

2.7 PREDICTION AND PREPARATION: In True/False question tasks it is sometimes possible to **predict** the likely correct answers based on either your common knowledge or on logic. (Of course, it is impossible to determine beforehand if something is <u>not</u> given.)

Look at the questions in Exercises 2.8 and 2.9 and try to predict what you will hear on the tape. Ask yourself:

- who is talking and possibly to whom?
- what is the topic that is to be discussed?

Circle the keywords and phrases to listen for. Guess the answers to the True/False/ Not Given questions **before** you listen, and later check your accuracy.

2.8 TRUE / FALSE / NOT GIVEN: Listen to Lecture 2 on the tape:

a.	We live in the most technologically advanced period in history.	**T F NG**
b.	Greenpeace will probably continue to keep a close watch on government policies.	**T F NG**
c.	The levels of Greenhouse gases will soon decrease.	**T F NG**
d.	The environment was not always considered an important political issue.	**T F NG**
e.	'Green' parties are mainly supported by young voters.	**T F NG**
f.	Hardwood forests are being destroyed for long-term profit.	**T F NG**
g.	The best recipe for environmental protection is poverty.	**T F NG**
h.	Technology and economic growth assist conservation.	**T F NG**
i.	There will soon be soon be cheaper food and cleaner cars.	**T F NG**
j.	The environment will benefit if we help the economy to grow.	**T F NG**

2.9 SHORT-ANSWER QUESTIONS: Refer to Lecture 2 on the tape.
All the answers below have a *MAXIMUM NUMBER OF FOUR WORDS*:

i. At the start of the new millenium, what is beginning to be reversed?

....

ii. Two 'watchdog' organisations are named. Greenpeace and

....

iii. According to the speaker, what is the most encouraging sign?

....

iv. What is given as a direct cause of 'environmental ruin'?

....

v. Which high-tech solution is given that will conserve natural resources?

....

(ANSWERS ON PAGE 114)

◢ READING EXERCISES 2.1 - 2.11

☺ **2.1 PREDICTION:** Look at the illustration below and the words and phrases taken from the Reading Passage on the next page. With a partner if possible, try to predict exactly what is being discussed:

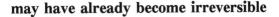

have not seen one

development of once natural areas

coming environmental disaster

theory

sensitive to environmental
variations in temperature

disappearing from rainforests

losing the ecological battle

species

at a loss to explain

no obvious reasons why

increase in ultraviolet radiation

upsetting the breeding cycles

warning us of a catastrophe

temperature increases

may have already become irreversible

☺ **2.2 PRE-READING QUESTIONS:** Before reading the text on the following page, work with a partner and ask and answer the questions below. Base your answers on your possible knowledge of the topic:

❒ What words would you use to describe frogs and toads?

❒ Why do you think one is less likely to come across a frog these days?

❒ What are the usual colours of frogs? Why?

❒ How might frogs be warning us of climate changes?

❒ Do you know what role frogs play in the ecological cycle of life?

❒ What do you think could be causing the disappearance of frogs?

Next, reorder the words in the mystery questions below:

1. **environment changes a it adapt Is can in the possible to species that ?**

    ....

2. **the you protects ozone what from the layer do know Earth ?**

    ....

2.3 SKIMMING: Read the text once for the gist (overall idea) and then in detail:

para.1 When was the last time you saw a frog? Chances are, if you live in a city, you have not seen one for some time. Even in wet areas once teeming with frogs and toads, it is becoming less and less easy to find those slimy, hopping and sometimes poisonous members of the animal kingdom. All over the world, even in remote jungles on the far side of the globe,
5 frogs are losing the ecological battle for survival, and biologists are at a loss to explain their demise. Are amphibians simply over-sensitive to changes in the ecosystem? Could their rapid decline in numbers be signalling some coming environmental disaster for us all?

para.2 This frightening scenario is in part the consequence of a dramatic increase over the last quarter century in the development of once natural areas of wet marshland; home not
10 only to frogs but to all manner of wildlife. Yet, there are no obvious reasons why certain frog species are disappearing from rainforests in the Southern Hemisphere which are barely touched by human hand. The mystery is unsettling to say the least, for it is known that amphibian species are extremely sensitive to environmental variations in temperature and moisture levels. The danger is that planet Earth might not only lose a vital link in the
15 ecological food chain (frogs keep populations of otherwise pestilent insects at manageable levels), but we might be increasing our output of air pollutants to levels that may have already become irreversible. Frogs could be inadvertently warning us of a catastrophe.

para.3 An example of a bizarre occurrence regarding a species of frog dates from the summer of 1995, when 'an explosion' of multi-coloured frogs of the species _Rana klepton esculenta_
20 occurred in the Netherlands. Normally these frogs are brown and greenish-brown, but some unknown contributory factor is turning these frogs yellow and/or orange. Nonetheless, so far, the unusual bi- and even tri-coloured frogs are functioning similarly to their normal-skinned contemporaries. It is thought that frogs with lighter coloured skins might be more likely to survive in an increasingly warm climate due to global warming.

para.4 One theory put forward to explain extinct amphibian species that seems to fit the facts concerns the depletion of the ozone layer, a well-documented phenomenon which has led to a sharp increase in ultraviolet radiation levels. The ozone layer is meant to shield the Earth from UV rays, but increased radiation may be having a greater effect upon frog populations than previously believed. Another theory is that worldwide temperature
30 increases are upsetting the breeding cycles of frogs.

2.4 WORD DEFINITIONS: Find the single words in paragraphs 1 and 2 which mean the following:

i.   appearing in great numbers ....   iv. death   ....

ii. disturbing   ....   v.   deterioration   ....

iii. unintentionally   ....   vi. branch of biology (adj.) ....

Next, find the single words in paragraphs 3 and 4 which mean the following:

i.   no longer in existence   ....   iv. (beings) existing at   ....
                                                   the same time

ii. remarkable occurrence   ....   v.   strange, weird, odd ....

iii. assisting   ....   vi. (to) protect   ....

2.5 TEXT ANALYSIS:

i. Choose the best heading for each paragraph in the passage from Exercise 2.3:

a) The mystery of amphibian decline.
b) Frogs making changes to the ecosystem.
c) Multi-coloured frog species cause problems
d) Frogs declining in number.
e) Theories concerning the demise of frogs.
f) Possible adaption of frogs to the environment.
g) Proof that global warming is harmful.
h) Fewer frogs in wet marshland.
i) An example of the extinction of a frog species.

Paragraph 1   ....   Paragraph 3   ....

Paragraph 2   ....   Paragraph 4   ....

ii. What would the next paragraph to follow the passage probably be about?

a) Searching for other multi-coloured frogs.

b) Feeding habits of frogs.

c) What is being done to reduce the problem.

d) Other forms of wildlife at risk.

iii. To what do the following pronouns in the passage refer?

a) one   *(line 2)*   ....

b) their   *(line 7)*   ....

c) these   *(line 20)*   ....

d) their   *(line 22)*   ....

2.6 GAPFILL: Below is a summary of part of the passage in Exercise 2.3. Choose words from the box below and refer to the passage to fill the gaps. First, name the parts of speech of the missing words:

The decline in the numbers of frogs worldwide may be (1)............... us of a coming ecological (2)................ . It might already be too late to (3)............... the trend. Frogs are becoming increasingly (4)............... to find partly because their natural habitat is being lost to (5)............... . Yet this does not explain why frogs are also (6)............... from areas of unspoilt (7)............... . Frogs are highly (8)............... to temperature (9)............... and might adversely react to (10)............... changes long before we become aware of the threat.

Parts of speech: (1) ...*verb form (-ing)*... (2) .... (3) .... (4) ....
(5) .... (6) .... (7) .... (8) .... (9) .... (10) ....

mystery	due to	found	reverse	irreversible	warn
development	slimy	dangerous	teeming	rainforest	amphibians
numbers	warning	develop	chain	trend	sensitive
difficult	cities	easy	increase	signal	environmental
moisture	population	level	disaster	variations	disappearing

2.7 WORDS & PHRASES WITH SIMILAR MEANINGS: Refer to the passage in Exercise 2.3, and see page 126 for advice on recognising pattern types. Circle the appropriate pattern type in each case.

i.   worldwide   → *(para. 1)* .... (Pattern Type: **1   2   3**)

ii.   unable to explain   → *(para. 1)* .... (Pattern Type: **1   2   3**)

iii. amhibian species   → *(para. 2)* .... (Pattern Type: **1   2   3**)

iv. all kinds of wildlife   → *(para. 2)* .... (Pattern Type: **1   2   3**)

v.   extremely unusual   → *(para. 3)* .... (Pattern Type: **1   2   3**)

vi. suggested   → *(para. 4)* .... (Pattern Type: **1   2   3**)

vii. agree with what is known → *(para. 4)* .... (Pattern Type: **1   2   3**)

☺ **2.8 SPEED READING:** Look below at the first few sentences of the passage on frogs. The text has been divided up into naturally forming phrases, and the stressed syllables have been marked. **Practice speaking the text out loud**, paying attention to the meaning of each phrase, grouping the words in the phrase words together, and regulating the 'beat' of the stresses within the phrase.

Now **mark the natural phrases** and stresses in the rest of the passage in Exercise 2.3 and practice accordingly.

When was the last time you saw a frog? / Chances are, / if you live in a city, / you haven't seen a frog for some time. / Even in wet areas / once teeming with frogs and toads, / it is becoming less and less easy / to find those slimy, hopping and sometimes poisonous / members of the animal kingdom. / All over the world, / even in remote jungles on the far side of the globe, / frogs are losing the ecological battle for survival, / and biological scientists / are at a loss to explain their demise.

2.9 TRUE / FALSE / NOT GIVEN: Refer to the text in Exercise 2.3.

a.   Frogs are disappearing only from city areas.   **T   F   NG**

b.   Frogs and toads are usually poisonous.   **T   F   NG**

c.   Biologists are unable to explain why frogs are dying.   **T   F   NG**

d.   The frogs' natural habitat is becoming more and more developed.   **T   F   NG**

e.   Attempts are being made to halt the development of wet marshland.   **T   F   NG**

f.   Frogs are important in the ecosystem because they control pests.   **T   F   NG**

g.   It is not known why the Netherlands frogs are changing colour.   **T   F   NG**

h.   Highly-coloured frogs are an unusual phenomenon in nature.   **T   F   NG**

i.   The multi-coloured frogs are exhibiting abnormal behaviour.   **T   F   NG**

j.   There is convincing evidence that the ozone layer is being depleted.   **T   F   NG**

k.   It is a fact that frogs' breeding cycles are upset by worldwide increases in temperature.   **T   F   NG**

2.10 SHORT-ANSWER QUESTIONS: Answer the following questions with words and phrases taken from the passage in Exercise 2.3.

i. From paragraph 1, name THREE places from which frogs are disappearing:

1. ....

2. ....

3. ....

ii. Name the TWO mentioned dangers to the Earth because of decreasing frog numbers:

1. ....

2. ....

iii. What might frogs require to be more likely to survive global warming? *(MAXIMUM OF THREE WORDS)*

....

iv. What has led to an increase in UV radiation? *(MAXIMUM OF THREE WORDS)*

....

v. What is the total number of reasons and theories given to explain disappearing frogs?

....

2.11 CROSSWORD: Refer to the Part 2 Listening Passages and the Reading Passage (and questions) for all answers.

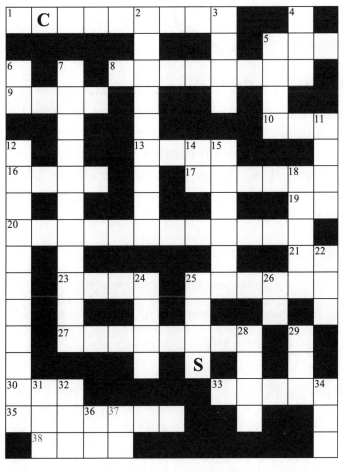

Across:
1. biologically interactive system (n)
5. (to) suit, be in agreement with (v)
8. not destroyed, pure (adj)
9. a 'mud ----' is an area of wasteland (n)
10. not dry (adj)
13. an amphibian (n)
16. "planes ---- -diving into the sea" (n)
17. waste material in a sewer (n)
19. meaning 'again' (prefix)
20. cannot be changed back again (adj)
21. '-- least' means 'minimally' (prep)
23. not the whole (n)
25. not close, very far away (adj)
27. (to) put in danger (v)
30. full form of ' n't ' (adj)
33. (and 6 and 29 down) explosion of flammable substance (3 words) (n)
35. wheel driven by water or gas (n)
38. (see 3 down)

Down:
2. very easily affected by something (adj)
3. (and 38 across) movement of water caused by a heavenly body
4. pack of various parts for project (n)
5. (to) move slowly, gracefully (v)
6. (see 33 across)
7. disaster (n)
11. large plant (n)
12. surroundings (n)
14. 'as well --' or also
15. death (n)
18. very large (adj)
22. number (adj)
24. (to) catch (v)
25. platforms for drilling oil in the sea (n)
26. (and 28 down) (to) depend on (v)
28. (see 26 down)
29. (see 33 across)
31. not in (adj)
32. three (prefix)
34. a couple (n)
36. Biology Dept. (initials)
37. that is (abbrev.)

(ANSWERS ON PAGE 114)

✍ WRITING EXERCISES 2.1 - 2.8

😐 2.1 A DESCRIPTION OF HOW SOMETHING WORKS:

Writing Task 1 might ask you to describe how a machine or object works, or how it is used for a particular purpose. Look at the bicycle below and, with a partner if possible, discuss how the labelled parts assist with its function:

The bicycle is a relatively recent invention. It is by far the most economical and environmentally-friendly mechanical mode of transport yet invented.

Describe how the illustrated two-wheeled bicycle below functions, and be sure to mention in your description the machine's environmentally-friendly feature. *

(* You are sure to lose marks if you omit to mention this feature)

2.2 HOW TO APPROACH THE TASK: Writing Task 1:

A. First, it is necessary to <u>describe the function that the machine or object is designed to perform</u>. Although it might be quite obvious what the function is, your job when writing a description is to be as informative as possible; you are not completing the task if you fail to tell the reader what the machine or object actually does. You should assume that the reader knows nothing at all about the machine or object you are looking at.

> Some ways to begin describing **the function** of a machine or object:
>
> The illustration is of a .... which is designed to *(do something)*.
>
> A .... is a .... designed for the purpose of *(doing something)*.
>
> The function of a .... is to *(do something)*.

Now write the introductory (topic) sentence of the description of the bicycle illustrated above:

....

....

....

B. Next, <u>inform the reader of the parts that make up the machine or object</u>.

Ways to describe the **component parts** of a machine or object:

A	is made up of	..*(how many?)...*	main	parts. *
	consists of	a number of	distinct	sections. *
	comprises		separate	

* Note that you can place a colon here, in which case you would <u>not</u> follow the colon with a capital letter. You may then list the parts by separating them with commas as follows:

... parts: a .... , a .... , a .... , and a ....
... sections:

Alternatively, you may start a new sentence after the full stop:

First, there is the .... Then the .... , the .... and the ....

Now write a sentence describing the parts that make up a bicycle:

....

....

....

....

C. After drawing attention to the parts that make up the machine or object, the next step is to <u>describe how those parts function together</u>. To do this, it is normal to use the Passive Voice, since it avoids the use of unnecessary references to whom or what is using the machine or object. However, it is sometimes necessary to refer to the person or thing using the machine at least once, usually at the beginning of the description of how it is being used. In this case, we need to <u>know how to refer to the active participant</u>.

Ways to refer to **the active participant(s)** of the machine or object:

   1.   YOU   i.e. First, you put your .... on the ....

   2.   WE *   i.e. First, we put our .... on the ....

   3.   THE (USER) i.e. First, (the cyclist) puts his or her .... on the ....

   4.   ONE *   i.e. First, one puts one's .... on the ....

* Note that it is not usually a good idea to refer to the active participant as 'we'. It is less formal. On the other hand, the use of 'one' can be rather too formal and affected.

The best way in which to refer to the active participant is to use a <u>single</u> individual (the cyclist, the operator etc.) to refer to <u>all</u> users. Of course, the problem of references to the user is avoided with use of the Passive Voice.

Now complete the description of the bicycle by inserting references to the active participant and by inserting suitable passive constructions in the following gapfill. Choose from the box of words and phrases below the gapfill text. Also, insert the names of the various parts of the machine as labelled in the illustration on page 30.

Note that not all the words and phrases in the box or in the illustration may be placed in this text:

The (1)_____ , who (2)_____ on top of a (3)_____ covered by a soft (4)_____ , leans forwards and grips the (5)_____ , pushing down with his or her feet on the (6)_____ which rotate up and down. They drive a central (7)_____ which (8)_____ by a (9)_____ to the back (10)_____ .

Alternative gear positions are available by operating a (11)_____ at hand level. Also on the handlebars is the (12)_____ which (13)_____ by a (14)_____ to a (15)_____ on the back wheel.

Accessories include an (16)_____ , with which the (17)_____ (18)_____ periodically with air, a (19)_____ , and a (20)_____ for use at night.

is connected	cyclist	are located	you	are filled
one	is driven	is linked	is balanced	are moved
are attached	we	driver	are pushed	is seated

2.3 LAYOUT: Writing Task 1.

Carefully read the '10 Point Guide to Presentation and Layout' on page 127 (reprinted from *'101 Helpful Hints for IELTS'*) before writing out the complete description of the bicycle (from Exercises 2.1 and 2.2) on the lines below. Pay particular attention to the way in which you separate your paragraphs. (Are you using the modern or traditional method?) Check the layout of the model answer in the Answer Key on page 115.

WRITING TASK 1:

....

....

....

....

....

....

WRITING TASK 1 - continued:

....

....

....

....

....

....

....

....

....

....

....

....

....

....

....

....

2.4 THE TOPIC & THE TOPIC QUESTION: Writing Task 2:

Circle the topic and write the topic question as a 'wh' or yes/no question:

Example: **'Describe some of the problems that (overpopulation) causes and suggest at least one possible solution.'**

What are the problems that (it) causes? What is one possible solution?

a. To what extent is recycling domestic waste beneficial? Discuss ways in which a householder can help to conserve valuable resources.

....

b. The government should spend more on public transport and discourage private car ownership to reduce air pollution in major cities. Do you agree or disagree?

....

c. Smoking should be allowed in public places. Smokers have rights too. How far do you agree with this statement?

....

2.5 LINKING AND SEQUENCING WORDS: Writing Task 2:
Your college tutor has asked you to write a short essay on the following topic:

'Describe some of the problems that overpopulation causes and suggest at least one possible solution.'

WRITING TASK 2 - Model Answer: Add linking and sequencing words from the box below:

para.1 In most countries of the world the population is increasing alarmingly. This is especially true in poor, undeveloped countries. Overpopulation causes a considerable number of problems.

para.2 In poor countries it is difficult to provide enough food to feed even the present number of people. (1)_____ , education to limit the number of children per family is not always successful. Poorer countries usually have a lot of unemployment (2)_____ , (3)_____ an increase in population simply makes the situation worse. The environment (4)_____ suffers when there are too many people living on the land.

para.3 In rich, industrialised and developing countries it is very difficult for governments to provide effective public services in overcrowded cities. (5)_____ , there is usually a great deal more crime, which is often due to high rates of unemployment. Further large increases in population only cause more overcrowding, unemployment and crime.

para.4 There are two main solutions to the overpopulation problem. (6)_____ , every woman who is pregnant but who does not want to give birth should be allowed by law to have an abortion. (7)_____ , governments must educate people to limit the size of the family. In China, couples are penalised financially if they have more than one child. This may seem cruel, (8)_____ the "one-child policy" is beginning to have an effect in the world's most populous nation. (9)_____ , similar policies might (10)_____ be necessary in other crowded nations, such as India (11)_____ .

para.5 (12)_____ , if the population explosion continues, many more people will die of starvation in poor countries, (13)_____ life in the cities, even in affluent nations, will become increasingly difficult.

and (x2)	....	**too**	....	**eventually**	....
in addition	....	**moreover**	....	**to sum up**	....
secondly	....	**also** (x2)	....	**firstly**	....
but	....	**for example**			

2.6 ARTICLES: Next, cover the model answer above and add the missing articles where necessary to the following sentences taken from the answer:

a.   In most (1)_____ countries of (2)_____ world (3)_____ population is increasing alarmingly. This is especially true in (4)_____ poor, undeveloped countries. (5)_____ overpopulation causes (6)_____ considerable number of (7)_____ problems.

b.   (8)_____ poorer countries usually have a lot of (9)_____ unemployment too, and (10)_____ increase in (11)_____ population simply makes (12)_____ situation worse. (13)_____ environment suffers when there are too many (14)_____ people living on (15)_____ land.

c. There are (16)_____ two main solutions to (17)_____ overpopulation problem. Firstly, every (18)_____ woman who is pregnant but who does not want to give (19)_____ birth should be allowed by (20)_____ law to have (21)_____ abortion.

d. (22)_____ "one-child policy" is beginning to have (23)_____ effect in (24)_____ world's most populous nation. Eventually, (25)_____ similar policies might also be necessary in (26)_____ other crowded nations, such as (27)_____ India for example.

2.7 SCRAMBLED SENTENCES: Without looking at Exercise 2.4, unscramble the following sentences taken from the model answer:

a. the present number | to feed | of people | to provide | even | in poor countries | enough food | difficult | it is

    ....

b. child | have | than | are | one | they | if | more | China | financially | couples | in | penalised

    ....

c. for governments | public services | developing countries | overcrowded cities | it is | and | rich industrialised | to provide | very difficult | in | in | effective

    ....

d. cause | large | more | unemployment | population | further only | in | and | overcrowding | increases | crime

    ....

2.8 PREPOSITIONS AND PUNCTUATION: Add the missing prepositions and punctuate these sentences from the passage in Exercise 2.4:

a. (1)_____ poor countries it is difficult (2)_____ provide enough food (3)_____ feed even the present number (4)_____ people

b. moreover there is usually a great deal more crime which is often due (5)_____ high rates (6)_____ unemployment further large increases (7)_____ population only cause more overcrowding unemployment and crime

c. governments must educate people (8)_____ limit the size (9)_____ the family

d. if the population explosion continues many more people will die (10)_____ starvation (11)_____ poor countries and life (12)_____ the cities even (13)_____ affluent nations will become increasingly difficult

(ANSWERS ON PAGE 114 - 115)

❋ SPELLING EXERCISES 2.1 - 2.2

2.1 SPELLING ERRORS: Locate all the spelling errors in the following sentences and correct them:

a. Studing a langauge in a contry wehre it is widly spoeken has meny advaintages.

....

b. Most oversees studnts lern Engerish at secondry skool or at unversity nowdays.

....

c. There knowlege of grammer is offen quiet advansed wich is certanly usefull when foriegners come to life in an Inglesh-spekin envirenment.

....

d. In Britain their are many oppurtunitys to practice liserning to and speking Engriss.

....

e. It is prefferable to mak frends with a nativ speakar in owder to practess connvesaton.

....

f. A resonable leval of English can be acheived quikly if a studnt is dedecated to studdy.

....

2.2 CORRECT SPELLING?: Only some of the following words are spelt correctly. Circle those that are incorrect and spell them properly below:

abreviation academic ackomplish aquisition adaption adminestration

....

analisis approch apropriate approximate assesment assingment

....

associated bibligraphy budget chronalogical classiffy campuss comunnication

....

comparitively comprehensiv comprize conclusion contekst coresspond councellor

....

criticism curicullum deadline diplomer discipline discushion drawback

....

ecornomic efficient eligibel emphasise enrollment esssential evalurate

....

evidense facillity faculty foundaton genneraly immprovise inadeqate

....

(ANSWERS ON PAGE 115)

❋ GRAMMAR EXERCISES 2.1 - 2.7

2.1 VERB FORMS (1): Complete each of the following sets of verb forms.

First, look at the following example:

live   ...*lived*....   ...*lived*....

REGULAR VERBS:

A affect	....	....	educate	....	....	help	....	....
believe	....	....	enjoy	....	....	join	....	....
....	climbed	....	....	....	escaped	....	....	kicked
connect	....	....	....	flowed	....	....	submitted	....
drop	....	....	....	happened	....	wait	....	....

IRREGULAR VERBS:

B be	....	....	go	....	....	speak	....	....
bring	....	....	....	had	....	....	shrank	....
....	....	driven	sleep	....	....	....	taught	....
eat	....	....	shoot	....	....	think	....	....
....	flew	....	....	....	struck	....	wrote	....

C	bought	....	feel	....	....	....	put	....
catch	....	....	....	found	....	spring	....	....
cut	....	....	meet	....	....	....	....	swum
....	....	cost	....	ran	....	wake	....	....
draw	....	....	sit	....	....	....	wound	

D awake	....	....	....	fled	....	....	made	....
....	....	done	....	....	forecasted	ring	....	....
dream	....	....	hang	....	....	spoil	....	....
....	fell	....	....	heard	....	....	swung	....
fight	....	....	....	....	known	weep	....	....

2.2 VERB FORMS (2): Complete the following sentences with the correct verb form(s). Note that two or more answers may be possible:

i.   Yesterday, I (see) .... the professor who (help) .... me with my survey results.

ii. In my life I (live) .... in many places, but I (think) .... the city lifestyle is best.

iii. The worst aspect of corporation policy (be) .... the disregard for the environment.

iv. It (be)............... previously important for a family to (own) .... their own home.

v.   In the 1990s, the government (introduce) .... special policies to (provide) .... funding for environmentalists to (continue) .... their work.

vi. Most environmental problems arise because discussions between warring factions (fail) .... to (bring about) .... realistic solutions.

vii. Throughout history it (not be) .... thought important to consider pollution issues.

viii. I believe governments should always be willing to (compromise) .... with those who (not want)............... the environment to be further damaged.

ix. There are two main reasons why it (be) .... always best to think before you buy.

x.   Last year, the amount of waste (increase) .... dramatically from 10% to over 35.5%.

2.3 CONDITIONAL TENSES: Complete the diagram below with the appropriate grammatical description or phrase from the large box below:

Conditional Type

Zero: If + [   ] ... , + present simple tense ...   + infinitive ...

1st: If + [   ] ... , + [   ] ... + infinitive ...

2nd: If + [   ] ... , + [   ] ... + infinitive ...

3rd: If + [   ] ... , + [   ] ... + [   ]

* note that '**unless**' is used to mean '**if not**'.

present	**simple continuous**	**tense (x 2)**	**past participle**	**past**	**simple continuous**	**tense**

will/may/might/can/must/should etc.

or **would might could** | **have**

would/might/could etc.

past perfect tense

2.4 WHICH CONDITIONAL?: Decide to which conditional type the following sentences belong - **Zero**, **1st**, **2nd**, **3rd**, or **mixed**. The first one has been done as an example:

i.   If governments are serious about saving hardwood forests, logging should be banned.

ii.   What would you do if you were the Minister for the Environment?

iii.   If we wish to protect the blue whale, we must encourage whaling nations to limit culls.

iv.   Endangered bird species will most likely become extinct, unless a solution to problems with their particular habitats is found.

v.   If aircraft noise levels are not dealt with, people who live close to airports will revolt.

vi.   If you are going to the beach this summer, would you mind not removing any seashells?

vii.   If money is not spent on prevention, governments will have to spend more in the end.

viii.   If enough wood fires are burnt in winter, air quality deteriorates rapidly.

ix.   You would not have eaten that fish if you had known it was caught in that river.

x.   Most people would be surprised if they knew what was added to their water supply.

xi.   If we want to lessen air pollution, we could start by banning smoking in public places.

xii.   Unless atmospheric temperature increases are controlled, sea levels will continue to rise.

i. *mixed*	iv.	vii.	x. ....
ii.	v.	viii.	xi. ....
iii.	vi.	ix.	xii. ....

2.5 PLURAL OR SINGULAR NOUNS?: Choose either the plural or singular form of the word in brackets:

i. The number of women involved *(was/were)* greater than the number of men.
ii. In the table, the figure refers to the females and *(is/are)* larger than the figure for males.
iii. The people who *(is/are)* at risk *(is/are)(that/those)* in the group that*(lives/live)* locally.
iv. The proportion of cars which *(use/uses)* unleaded petrol *(is/are)* smaller than that of all other cars.
v. The team of scientists *(was/were)* made up of biologists, geologists, and anthropologists.
vi. A plague of insects, which *(was/were)* destroying the farmland, *(was/were)* eliminated.
vii. The data from the earlier surveys *(is/are)* less reliable than the latest data.

2.6 PROPER NOUNS?: Find all the proper nouns in the text below and **capitalise** them. There are exactly 40 changes to be made:

1 A report in an australian daily newspaper, the sydney morning herald (tuesday may 28), reveals that sydney's air is fast becoming unfit to breathe. Researchers at the university of sydney claim that the benefits ensuing from the removal of lead from petrol have been largely offset by an increase in other harmful air pollutants.

5 Research conducted by dr. michael dawson and dr. brent young of the university's chemistry department, and partly based on surveys taken in britain, concludes that levels of benzene in the air are now a major health concern. An environmental consultant, mr. noel child, believes that breathing sydney's air is equivalent to smoking ten cigarettes a day.

However, according to the new south wales environment protection authority, current
10 levels of benzene in the city's air are not a cause for concern and air pollution levels are stable. The position taken by the authority would seem to be highly questionable given that another government department, the nsw roads and traffic authority, disclosed in the same report that there had been a 12-15% increase in traffic on sydney's major roads in the past year. *(international environment association - july 1998)*

2.7 AVOIDING NOUN REPETITION: The following words are used to avoid repetition of a noun or noun phrase in a sentence:

it, its, they, them, their, those, these, that, this, (do) so

Decide **exactly which words or phrases** the italicised words in the following passage are substituting for, and underline them:

1 The entire ecological system on Earth can be thought of as one huge living organism. *It* is composed of an infinitesimal number of interdependent units *that* all play *their* part in contributing to the well-being and functioning of the whole. We human beings are, of course, a part of *this* intricate web of life. Unfortunately, we often forget we are
5 inextricably linked to nature, and by *doing so*, inadvertently contribute to *its* slow destruction. Survival will depend on our willingness to reorganise our political thinking.

No longer can *those* who ignore nature's warnings continue to bury *their* heads in the sand. Unless *these* politicians (who, in democratic countries, are supposed to listen to the people as well as to corporations) do something about the enormous environmental
10 problems facing the Earth, *they* will cease to be respected, and *this* will mean our old systems of government will inevitably change and collapse. Nothing can save *them*.

(ANSWERS ON PAGES 115 - 116)

★ VOCABULARY EXERCISES 2.1 - 2.3

2.1 SUFFIXES (1): Certain suffixes indicate that the word is a **noun**, an **adjective**, a **verb** or an **adverb**. Sort the suffixes below into the correct boxes according to the parts of speech they indicate:

-al	-ment	-ous	-fy	-tion	-ic	-ist	-ness
-ly	-er	-ise (-ize)	-ish	-ive	-ism	-ship	-ate

Noun Indicators	Adjective Indicators
Verb Indicators	**Adverb Indicators**

2.2 SUFFIXES (2): Can you think of three of words ending in each of the suffixes listed in the exercise above?

2.3 WORD FORMATION: Complete the chart to provide the correct form of the words shown for the given parts of speech: (Not all forms are possible.)

NOUNS			ADJECTIVE	VERB	ADVERB
PLACE *	PERSON	GERUND/THING			
				pollute	
environment		-		-	
-			destructive		
-	-	prevention			-
				conserve	
-				-	protectively
	-	penalty			-
	-	disaster		-	
-	-		various		
nature		-		-	
-	-		specific		

* double word nouns are possible

(ANSWERS ON PAGE 116)

▰ LISTENING EXERCISES 3.1 - 3.9

3.1 SPEED LISTENING: Note only the essential details of what you hear: (Refer to the tapescript for confirmation.)

a. Manchester, ...

b. Situated ....

c. Technological ....

d. Unfortunately ....

e. The rise ....

f. Eventually ....

g. Liverpool ....

h. The Liverpool docks ....

i. ....

j. ....

3.2 NUMBERS AND LETTERS: (Refer to the tapescript for confirmation.)

A i. .... ii. .... iii. .... iv. .... v. ....

vi. .... vii. .... viii. .... ix. .... x. ....

B i. .... ii. .... iii. .... iv. ....

v. .... vi. .... vii. .... viii. ....

ix. .... x. ....

C i. .... ii. .... iii. .... iv. ....

v. .... vi. .... vii. .... viii. ....

ix. .... x. ....

D i. .... ii. .... iii. .... iv. .... v. ....

vi. .... vii. .... viii. .... ix. .... x. ....

3.3 GENERAL INFORMATION: Listen to Radio Items 5 & 6 and complete the chart with the basic details: (Refer to the tapescript for confirmation.)

	What?	Where?	When?	Who?	How?	Why?
Radio Item 5						
Radio Item 6						

3.4 GAPFILL: Listen to Radio Item 5 again and complete the gaps in the summary of the passage below with the correct word or phrase you hear:

An electronic (1)................ giving information on more than (2)................ of the actors registered in Britain, is now available on CD-ROM. Some theatrical (3)................ have over (4)................ actors on their books and it is difficult to remember all their details. The database lists information on over (5)................ actors and can be searched for details such as past (6)................ they have appeared in, special skills they might have, and even the colour of their (7)................ . The database can quickly locate persons with particular (8)................ and, although some actors feel it is too impersonal to be of much use, it is certain to change the way actors are chosen for (9)................ in theatrical shows. Ring the following telephone number for further enquiries on the product: (10)................ .

3.5 MULTIPLE CHOICE QUESTIONS: Listen to Radio Item 6 a second time and answer the following questions:

i.   The size of the sound device is:

   a) twice that of the remote control

   b) half that of the remote control

   c) about the size of one's thumb

   d) bigger than your thumb

ii. The only problem with the device is:

   a) the remote must be pointed at the TV

   b) it is expensive

   c) the sound levels cannot be preset

   d) the sound cannot be cut out completely

iii. Susan believes the device would:

   a) not sell well

   b) sell better than her other invention

   c) sell better if it was inside the TV

   d) none of the above

iv. The telephone answering machine:

   a) is called the 'Ad Subtractor'

   b) was invented by Susan's husband

   c) has sold very well

   d) automatically switches callers

3.6 SPECIFIC INFORMATION: Listen again to the radio items:

i.   What is the name of the show that tells of the latest software on CD-ROM?

ii. What is this particular CD-ROM called?

iii. Who would use this actor's directory?

iv. From where did Mr Harkney get the idea of a database of actors?

v.   Why are some actors unhappy about the concept of this database?

i.   What is the name of the show that looks at clever inventions?

ii. How long did it take to invent the sound reduction device?

iii. Why did Ms Schofield invent this device?

iv. Why do we not know how the device works?

v.   What other invention has Ms Schofield marketed?

3.7 DICTATION PREPARATION: In dictation exercises it is important not to get left behind. Although the IELTS Listening Sub-Test does not include a dictation, it is easy to get left behind and miss the answers to the next questions. This is usually because you are not fully prepared for what you are about to hear.

Look at the following words and phrases taken in sequence from the dictation in Exercise 3.8:

Modern world → threat → air → filtered → nose and lungs → big city → cigarettes → components → invisible gases → cannot smell → exhausts → cars → bloodstream → breath → future health → development → safer → engine.

What is the topic of the dictation text? Does it help you to know where the dictation is leading? Should you predict the direction of a listening? *(YES!)*

Use the dictation practice in the following exercise (Exercise 3.8) to practise moving on to the next phrase spoken, even if you miss the previous phrase.

3.8 DICTATION: Refer to Dictation 1 on the tape:

....
....
....
....
....
....
....
....
....
....

(Check your words, spelling and punctuation with the tapescript on page 105.)

3.9 TRUE / FALSE / NOT GIVEN: Listen to Lecture 3 on the tape:

a. Most people think the solution to city air pollution will be the electric or solar-powered car.   **T   F   NG**

b. According to the lecturer, solar-powered cars are impractical.   **T   F   NG**

c. The diesel engine was first produced in 1824.   **T   F   NG**

d. The diesel engine costs more to run.   **T   F   NG**

e. Diesel engines emit fewer air pollutants than petrol-driven engines.   **T   F   NG**

f. The new diesel engines will release poisonous nitrogen and oxygen.   **T   F   NG**

g. If all cars had diesel engines, traffic jams would disappear.   **T   F   NG**

h. Diesel engines are noisier and vibrate more.   **T   F   NG**

i. Car manufacturers were afraid that they would lose customers if they produced diesel-powered cars.   **T   F   NG**

(ANSWERS ON PAGE 117)

43

▧ READING EXERCISES 3.1 - 3.11

☺ **3.1 PREDICTION:** Look at the illustration below and the words and phrases taken from the Reading Passage on the next page. With a partner if possible, try to predict exactly what is being discussed:

anyone can set up a site

network

not owned or controlled by
any one organisation

young and old get connected

educational hope

latest technological revolution

communicate

linked

phone line

accessed for information

the future

freedom of access

not only text links ...
... but also graphs, images and even video

all over the world

potentially hazardous tool

☺ **3.2 PRE-READING QUESTIONS:** Before reading the text on the following page, work with a partner and ask and answer the questions below. Base your answers on your possible knowledge of the topic:

❐ Name various ways in which people communicate with each other long distance.

❐ How do you think people might communicate with each other in the future?

❐ Do you use a computer? What do you use it for?

❐ Have you ever used the Internet? What do you know about it?

❐ Why do you think some people fear the widespread use of the Internet?

❐ How does one move the cursor around the screen of a computer monitor?

Next, reorder the words in the mystery questions below:

1. **the get need to Internet What connected to do you ?**
   ....

2. **organisation an Internet by owned the Is ?**
   ....

3.3 SKIMMING: Read the text once for the gist (overall idea) and then in detail:

═══════════════

1 Almost everyone with or without a computer is aware of the latest technological revolution destined to change forever the way in which humans communicate, namely, the Information Superhighway, best exemplified by the ubiquitous Internet. Already, millions of people around the world are linked by computer simply by having a modem
5 and an address on the 'Net', in much the same way that owning a telephone links us to almost anyone who pays a phone bill. In fact, since the computer connections are made via the phone line, the Internet can be envisaged as a network of visual telephone links. It remains to be seen in which direction the Information Superhighway is headed, but many believe it is the educational hope of the future.

10 The World Wide Web, an enormous collection of Internet addresses or sites, all of which can be accessed for information, has been mainly responsible for the increase in interest in the Internet in the 1990s. Before the World Wide Web, the 'Net' was comparable to an integrated collection of computerised typewriters, but the introduction of the 'Web' in 1990 allowed not only text links to be made but also graphs, images and even video.

15 A Web site consists of a 'home page', the first screen of a particular site on the computer to which you are connected, from where access can be had to other subject related 'pages' at the site and to thousands of other computers all over the world. This is achieved by a process called 'hypertext'. By clicking with a mouse device on various parts of the screen, a person connected to the 'Net' can go travelling, or 'surfing' through
20 a web of pages to locate whatever information is required.

Anyone can set up a site; promoting your club, your institution, your company's products or simply yourself, is what the Web and the Internet is all about. And what is more, information on the Internet is not owned or controlled by any one organisation. It is, perhaps, true to say that no-one and therefore everyone owns the 'Net'. Because of
25 the relative freedom of access to information, the Internet has often been criticised by the media as a potentially hazardous tool in the hands of young computer users. This perception has proved to be largely false however, and the vast majority of users both young and old get connected with the Internet for the dual purposes for which it was intended - discovery and delight.

═══════════════

3.4 WORD DEFINITIONS: Find the single words in paragraphs 1 and 2 which mean the following:

i.   certain to become   ....   v.   complete change   ....

ii. a machine linking computers ....   vi. given as an example   ....

iii. found everywhere   ....   vii. location (of activity) ....

iv. interconnected group   ....   viii. vast, huge   ....

3.5 TEXT ANALYSIS:

i.   Which is the best title for the passage in Exercise 3.3?

   a) The World Wide Web   c) The Internet Revolution

   b) The Educational Hope of the Future   d) How to Use the Internet

ii. What is the main point of the first paragraph?

a) Almost everyone has heard of the Information Superhighway

c) You need a modem and an address to use the Internet

b) The Internet will revolutionise the way people communicate

d) No-one knows where the Information Superhighway is headed

iii. Which is the topic sentence of the second paragraph?

a) Sentence number one

c) The last sentence

b) Sentence number two

d) none of the above

iv. What would the next paragraph to follow the passage probably be about?

a) The future of the Internet

c) Abuse of the Internet by youth

b) Advertising on the World Wide Web

d) The cost of using the Internet

v. To what do the following pronouns in the passage refer?

a) it *(line 9)* ....

c) this *(line 17)* ....

b) which *(line 10)* ....

d) it *(line 28)* ....

3.6 GAPFILL: The following is a summary of the passage in Exercise 3.3. Choose words from the box below and refer to the passage to fill the gaps:

The Internet is the best (1).............. of the technological revolution known as the Information Superhighway. Linked by computer through global (2).............. lines, users can (3).............. obtain information by connecting to the World Wide Web. Before the 'Web', only (4).............. information could be flashed upon the computer (5)..............., but thanks to a process called (6)..............., visual images can easily be (7).............. by (8).............. through a maze of connected (9).............. on Web sites all over the world. The Internet is not independently (10)..............., which ensures freedom of access to information.

communicate	speedily	visual	computer	advertise	owned
example	hypertext	telephone	exemplified	screen	link
modem	travelling	textual	information	accessed	click
access	criticised	mouse	typewriter	only	pages

3.7 WORDS & PHRASES WITH SIMILAR MEANINGS: Refer to the passage in Exercise 3.3, and see page 126 for advice on recognising pattern types. Circle the appropriate pattern type in each case.

i. joined by → *(para. 1)* .... (Pattern Type: **1 2 3**)

ii. telephone links → *(para. 1)* .... (Pattern Type: **1 2 3**)

iii. large group → *(para. 2)* .... (Pattern Type: **1 2 3**)

iv. negotiating a maze → *(para. 2)* .... (Pattern Type: **1 2 3**)

v. comprises → *(para. 2)* .... (Pattern Type: **1 2 3**)

vi. dangerous tool → *(para. 3)* .... (Pattern Type: **1 2 3**)

vii. most people on the 'Net' → *(para. 3)* .... (Pattern Type: **1 2 3**)

3.8 MATCHING SENTENCE HALVES: Refer to the text in Exercise 3.3 and match the halves of the given sentences together:

a. Having a modem and an Internet address ...   + ...

b. The introduction of the 'Web' on the Internet allows ...   + ...

c. By a process called 'hypertext' ...   + ...

d. The Internet has often been criticised ...   + ...

e. The vast majority of Internet users ...   + ...

f. It is unclear what the Information Superhighway ...   + ...

g. ... because young computer users have potentially hazardous tools.

h. ... 'surfing' through the 'Net' is possible.

i. ... thousands of other computers all over the world with a 'home page'.

j. ... will lead to in the future.

k. ... for allowing access to potentially dangerous information.

l. ... do not abuse the freedom of access to information.

m. ... as the educational hope of the future.

n. ... enables millions of people around the world to be linked by computer.

o. ... abuse the Internet for the purpose of discovery and delight.

p. ... a transfer of graphics and images on interconnected computers.

3.9 TRUE / FALSE / NOT GIVEN: Refer to the text in Exercise 3.3.

a. Everyone is aware of the Information Superhighway.   **T   F   NG**

b. Using the Internet costs the owner of a telephone extra money.   **T   F   NG**

c. Internet computer connections are made by using telephone lines.   **T   F   NG**

d. The World Wide Web is a network of computerised typewriters.   **T   F   NG**

e. According to the author, the Information Superhighway may be the future hope of education.   **T   F   NG**

f. The process called 'hypertext' requires the use of a mouse device.   **T   F   NG**

g. The Internet was created in the 1990s.   **T   F   NG**

h. The 'home page' is the first screen of a 'Web' site on the 'Net'.   **T   F   NG**

i. The media has often criticised the Internet because it is dangerous.   **T   F   NG**

j. The latest technological revolution will change the way humans communicate.   **T   F   NG**

3.10 SHORT-ANSWER QUESTIONS: Refer to the text in Exercise 3.3.

   i. Name the two stated purposes for which the Internet was created :

     1. ....

     2. ....

   ii. According to the passage, owning a telephone links us to whom?

     ....

   iii. According to the author, the Internet since 1990 can be thought of as:

     ....

   iv. The process called 'hypertext' requires the use of a certain device. What is it?

     ....

   v. What do companies advertise on the Internet?

     ....

   vi. According to the passage, who does the Internet belong to?

     ....

3.11 WORDSEARCH: All words are taken from the Part 3 Listening and Reading Passages. Match the words and meanings in boxes A and B on the left. Next, locate the words in the wordsearch grid. (Answers to the clues are upside down and back-to-front under the grid - hold them up to a mirror):

A
1. approach or way in (n) ......
2. thought of, imagined as (pp) ..*c*..
3. invention, thing designed for a particular function (n) ......
4. with two parts (adj) ......
5. hard to find or catch (adj) ......
6. (to) take away from something (v) ......

   a. (T R E C A D T)
   b. (E V D C E I)
   c. (E V I G N A D S E)
   d. (L E V I E U S)
   e. (C E C S A S)
   f. (U A D L)

B
7. small and clever device (n) ......
8. joined together (v) ......
9. electronic box that connects computers (n) ......
10. interconnected group (n) ......
11. plot of land, place where activity takes place (n) ......
12. equivalent of the big toe but on the hand (n) ......

   g. (R K O T N E W)
   h. (T E S I)
   i. (K N I L D E)
   j. (T A D G G E)
   k. (B H M T U)
   l. (O D M M E)

D	E	G	A	S	I	V	N	E
T	C	A	R	T	E	D	L	P
M	K	E	D	P	X	U	L	W
E	R	B	C	E	S	K	A	N
D	O	Z	M	I	K	Z	U	Y
O	W	U	V	U	V	N	D	S
M	T	E	G	R	H	E	I	L
T	E	G	D	A	G	T	D	L
J	N	B	S	S	E	C	C	A

6. DETRACT   12. THUMB
5. ELUSIVE   11. SITE
4. DUAL   10. NETWORK
3. DEVICE   9. MODEM
2. ENVISAGED   8. LINKED
1. ACCESS   7. GADGET

(Hold up to a mirror to view answers!)

(ANSWERS ON PAGE 117)

✍ WRITING EXERCISES 3.1 - 3.7

3.1 IDENTIFYING THE MAIN FEATURES: Writing Task 1:

Identify 10 key features of the information given in the bar chart for the example Writing Task 1 below. Complete the sentences below the bar chart.

The bar chart below shows the number of overseas students enrolled in a second year Graphic Design course at a college in the south of England.

Write a report for a university lecturer describing the information shown.

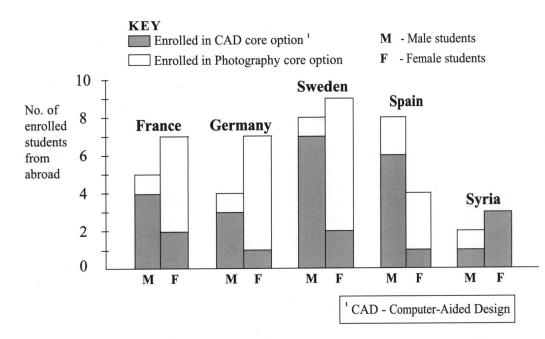

MAIN FEATURES:

1. More students are enrolled from .... than any other country.

2. The least number of students is enrolled from ....

3. The profiles of students from ..*France*..... and .... are similar.

4. More ...*female*...... than .... students are enrolled in the Design College.

5. Every country except .... has more female students enrolled in the College.

6. The country with the most females students enrolled is ....

7. More .... than .... students are enrolled in the Photography core option from every country except ....

8. Overall, more male students are enrolled in the .... core option.

9. Overall, more .... students are enrolled in the Photography core option.

10. No Syrian .... students are taking the Photography core option.

3.2 SENTENCE INSERTION: Practice for Writing Task 1:

Insert the statistical information from the graph in Exercise 3.1 into the blank spaces in the model answer on the following page and in the 'missing sentences' labelled 'a' to 'e'. Then, insert the 'missing' sentences into the model answer.

WRITING TASK 1 - Model Answer:

para.1 **(i)**... . Some students are enrolled in the Computer-Aided Design (CAD) core option; the others are taking Photography.

para.2 Overall, Sweden has the largest number of enrolled students ((1)_____) and Syria the smallest ((2)_____). **(ii)**... .

para.3 **(iii)**.. . For each nationality the males taking CAD outnumber the females, except in the case of the Syrians with (3)_____ females to only (4)_____ male. Sweden has the most students studying CAD ((5)_____); Spain is next with (6)_____ , while France has (7)_____ . Germany and Syria have (8)_____ CAD students each.

para.4 **(iv)**.. . In fact, no female Syrian students are taking Photographic Design. **(v)**... .

---

a. According to the bar chart, students from four European countries (Sweden, Spain, France and Germany) and one Middle Eastern country (Syria) are taking Graphic Design at the college.

b. Only (9)_____ male from each country is enrolled in Photography, except for (10)_____ males from Spain.

c. As for the photography option, more females than males are enrolled from every country except Syria.

d. Students from all five countries are enrolled in CAD, but more males are taking this option than females ((11)_____ and (12)_____ respectively).

e. France and Spain both have (13)_____ students; Germany has (14)_____ . It is noticeable that France and Germany have similar profiles.

3.3 THE TOPIC & THE TOPIC QUESTION: Writing Task 2:
Circle the topic and write the topic question as a 'wh' or yes/no question:

Example: *'To what extent is* (nuclear technology) *a danger to life on Earth? What are the benefits and risks associated with its use?'*

......*Is (it) a danger to life on Earth?*.................................

a. Computers are essential in the modern office these days. Write about the advantages and disadvantages of relying on computers to run a small business.

....

b. Advanced medical technology can extend the life of the sick and aged to well beyond the age of 70. Discuss the possible effects of increasing natural life-span.

....

c. Mobile phones have changed our lifestyle forever, but not all the changes are for the best. Discuss the pros and cons of owning a mobile phone.

....

3.4 INTRODUCTION: Writing Task 2:

A university lecturer has asked you to write an essay on the following topic:

'To what extent is nuclear technology a danger to life on Earth? What are the benefits and risks associated with its use?'

For the introduction, choose the **one correct phrase** from each column to form two correct sentences. All the other phrases result in incorrect English.

a.

Nowdays,	all people	are scared with	nuclear powers	because of
In this day,	many people	fear the use of	nuclear technology	the reason is
These days,	some of the people	are afraid of	nuclear weapons	this is because

… many dangers	associated with	this technology use.
… the dangers	joined to	its use.
… danger that is	of association	use this technology.

b.

According to me,	…
My belief that,	…
In my opinion,	…

c.

… although it is true	nuclear war	the greatest threat to life is,	the use of
… even if it is true	nuclear technology	is the great threat to life,	use of
… it is true	that nuclear weapons	pose the greatest threat to life,	the using

… nuclear technology	for peaceful use	too carries	lot of problem.
… it	for peaceful purposes	also carries	some certain risk.
… them	in times of war	takes as well	some serious risks.

3.5 BODY: Next, add the missing articles where necessary to form the **first two paragraphs** for the body of your answer:

a. (1)_____ nuclear power stations provide (2)_____ important source of (3)_____ cheap power for (4)_____ many industrialised nations and some (5)_____ developing countries. However, there is always (6)_____ danger of (7)_____ radiation leaking from these plants. Even though (8)_____ safety precautions are taken, there have been (9)_____ numerous disasters such as (10)_____ explosion of (11)_____ nuclear plant in (12)_____ Russia not long ago.

b. (13)_____ nuclear technology is even used to help cure (14)_____ some diseases such as (15)_____ cancer. (16)_____ radiation can be applied to (17)_____ body to burn away (18)_____ cancerous cells. This is, however, (19)_____ dangerous procedure and (20)_____ application of (21)_____ radiation is almost always painful and not always successful.

Next, identify the components of the **third** body paragraph:

c. The most worrying aspect of nuclear technology, though, is its use for military purposes. Enough atomic bombs have already been built to completely destroy the planet, and the real danger is that one day some country will start a war with these weapons. Too many countries now have the technology required to make such bombs, and there is currently much debate about how to control the situation.

What is the main topic idea? ....

Identify and underline the 3 supporting arguments.

The summary statement begins: ....

3.6 CONCLUSION: Next, choose the **one correct phrase** from each column to form the first two sentences of the conclusion.

a. At the end,   ...
    In conclusion,   ...
    The final opinion is, ...

b. ... nuclear technology certainly | has / had / did had | positive uses but | were / was / is | nonetheless dangerous.

c. However, it | is / would be / would have been | better if it | had never been / was never been / will be never | used to create nuclear weapons.

Next, unscramble the final summary sentence:

d. all | should agree | is to continue | to disarm | the nuclear nations | if | possible | life on Earth | as soon as | of the world.

....

3.7 LINKING AND SEQUENCING WORDS: Add the missing linking or sequencing words from the box below to form the completed model answer:

WRITING TASK 2 - Model Answer:

para.1 These days, many people are afraid of nuclear technology because of the dangers associated with its use. In my opinion, (1)_____ it is true that nuclear weapons pose the greatest threat to life, the use of nuclear technology for peaceful purposes also carries some serious risks.

para.2 Nuclear power stations provide an important source of cheap power for many industrialised nations and some developing countries. (2)_____ , there is always the danger of radiation leaking from these plants. (3)_____ safety precautions are taken, there have been numerous disasters (4)_____ the explosion of a nuclear plant in Russia not long ago.

para.3 Nuclear technology is even used to help cure some diseases (5)_____ cancer. Radiation can be applied to the body to burn away cancerous cells. This is, (6)_____ , a dangerous procedure (7)_____ the application of radiation is almost always painful (8)_____ not always successful.

para.4 The most worrying aspect of nuclear technology, (9)_____ , is its use for military purposes. Enough atomic bombs have already been built to completely destroy the planet, (10)_____ the real danger is that one day some country will start a war with these weapons. Too many countries now have the technology required to make such bombs (11)_____ there is currently much debate about how to control the situation.

para.5 (12)_____ , nuclear technology certainly has positive uses (13)_____ is nonetheless dangerous. (14)_____ , it would have been better if it had never been used to create nuclear weapons. If life on Earth is to continue, all the nuclear nations of the world should agree to disarm as soon as possible.

but	....	however (x3)	....	though	....
in conclusion	....	such as (x2)	....	and (x4)	....
even though	....	although	....		

(ANSWERS ON PAGES 117 - 118)

❋ SPELLING EXERCISES 3.1 - 3.2

3.1 SPELLING ERRORS:
All the following sentences contain spelling errors. First, find all the incorrectly spelt words. Next, **rank the sentences** in order according to the number of errors they contain (from 1 to 10 errors):

a. Computers are everywhere these days, not just on the desk top, but inside many off the electrical applliances we purrchase.

b. Tranzistorised compoter chipps can determmine owr preferrences for varouis settings on such macheens as microwaives, televizion sets, air-conditioning units, and, of course, cars.

c. One of the benefits of the proliferation of 'invisible' chips within machines is that so many of the repetetive tasks we must perform every day can be automated.

d. For exammple, a digitil memory of audio settings for CD playback can be invokked four faster settings next sesssion, and also use two compile 'songbooks' of personnel favurites.

e. Allso, garagge dorrs can open seconds before our car turns the corner into the driveway, and telefones can automatically divvert callers to preset destennations.

f. Soon, you might be able to programme video recourders to record what the machine 'thinks' is suittable for you to view, bassed on a short personality and prefference quiz.

g. Perhaps, the most important use to which these new robotic service technologys can be put is the conservation of energy resourses.

h. Water heeters and other power-drorring appliances can be monitered to minnimise energy consumtion by automaticaly plugging in to the community power grid at optimum times.

i. Naturrally, thees noo technologies are not without there detracters who usualy point out that the less hands-on control we have over a machine, the greater the marrgin for erorr.

j. Uthers, counter that these internal chips are pre-programmed and, therefore, can be more thoroghly checked, statisticaly prodducing far fewer errors then humans.

RANKING: ....

3.2 CORRECT SPELLING?:
Only some of the following words are spelt correctly. Circle those that are incorrect, and spell them properly below:

inovative   investigate   irrelevent   laborotory   lecture   literrally

....

ilogical   matereal   medier   minimun   monitor   negative

....

negotiate   noticable   organise   outline   persentage   parsuade   policy

....

postgradaute   postpon   prediction   preferrence   prosess   programe   proposition

....

(ANSWERS ON PAGE 118)

❋ GRAMMAR EXERCISES 3.1 - 3.6

3.1 RELATIVE CLAUSES (1): Decide if the underlined clauses in the sentences below are **defining** or **non-defining** clauses:

i.   The inventor of the wheel, who must have been a remarkably creative individual, probably got the idea from watching logs being used to transport materials.

ii. It was the printing press that was developed by Gutenburg in Germany that changed forever the process of writing, and not the invention by the Chinese.

iii. Unfortunately, the particular printing technique which was invented by the Chinese was doomed to be used for thousands of years by only a privileged few.

iv. Of all the inventions that have changed the world, surely the most influential was that of the motor car.

v.   The television, which was invented simultaneously by two persons working independently of each other, has certainly changed the way in which families communicate.

vi. It remains to be seen if computers, which are supposed to bypass the need for paper products, will yet be responsible for making the dream of the paperless office a reality.

What do you notice about the different **punctuation** used for defining and non-defining clauses?

3.2 RELATIVE CLAUSES (2): Add suitable **non-defining clauses** to the sentences below to make them more interesting to read:

i.   Technology, ... , is sometimes thought of as being extraordinarily complex.

ii. However, even the simple kite, ... , is an example of applied technology.

iii. In fact, we rarely think about most of the less complex technology in use, such as the door, ... , and the simple step, ...

iv. The more spectacular examples of modern technology, the telephone for example, ... , are completely taken for granted.

3.3 RELATIVE CLAUSES (3): Add suitable **defining clauses** to the following sentences to have them make more sense. Choose from the box below:

i.   Nobody .... can fully understand how television works.

ii. Genetic engineering is destined to change the way in which animals .... end up on the kitchen table.

iii. People .... are able to achieve what was technically impossible a short while ago.

iv. CDs .... are less expensive but are often unreliable.

v.   Software manufacturers take advantage of customers ....

that are farmed for food	**who are proficient with computers**
who is technologically ignorant	**that refuse to read the fine print**
which are manufactured in countries employing cheap labour	

3.4 CONDITIONAL SENTENCE COMPLETION: Complete the unfinished conditional sentences below with words you choose. (Look at the conditional structure grid in the Answer Key on page 116.)

Note that the sentence parts are not intended to be matched together.

If the world's wildlife is not better protected, ...

If parents refuse to discipline their children at home, ...

If the United Nations had acted sooner, ...

Unless gun ownership is severely restricted, ...

... , the money spent on computers in school may be wasted.

... , there would be a huge increase in the nation's health.

... , it could be a disaster for humankind.

If our sexual roles had been reversed, ...

If it were not for our police force, ...

....

....

....

....

....

....

....

....

....

3.5 COUNTABLE OR UNCOUNTABLE NOUNS?: Decide if the nouns or noun phrases below are countable, and make the verb agreement:

i.   The news of the latest silicon chip breakthroughs (*was/were*) very exciting.

ii. How much information about the planets (*is/are*) known?

iii. Because the human species (*is/are*) a cancerous growth on this planet, it is absurd to spend millions on 'in vitro fertilisation' techniques.

iv. A basic knowledge of mathematics (*is/are*) vital to a computer programmer.

v.   The politics of the higher technologies (*determine/determines*) which universities (*receive/receives*) funding.

vi. Petroleum is one of the earth's most precious resources and (*require/requires*) endless technological innovation to ensure (*its/their*) continued extraction from land or sea.

vii. Few people (*know/knows*) that nuclear power plants are less radioactive than coal mines.

(ANSWERS ON PAGE 118)

3.6 PHRASAL VERB GAME:

START: **Player 4**

Prepositions / adverbs (reference list):

through · back · forward · around · across · about · apart · away · by · round · to
at · in · on · off · up · down · against · for · with · out · over
in · into

START: **Player 1** · START: **Player 2** · START: **Player 3**

PREPOSITION OR ADVERB → VERB ↓	1	2	3	4	5	6	7	8	9	10	11	12	13
be	bell	o	o	o	o	o	o	o	o	o	o	o	bell
break	o	o	book	book	o	o	o	o	o	book	book	o	o
bring	o	o	book	book	o	o	o	o	o	book	book	o	o
come	o	o	o	o	o	o	o	o	o	o	o	o	o
get	o	o	o	o	o	o	o	o	o	o	o	o	o
go	o	o	o	o	o	bottle	bottle	bottle	o	o	o	o	o
look	o	o	o	o	o	bottle	bottle	bottle	o	o	o	o	o
make	o	o	o	o	o	bottle	bottle	bottle	o	o	o	o	o
put	o	o	o	o	o	o	o	o	o	o	o	o	o
see	o	o	o	o	o	o	o	o	o	o	o	o	o
set	o	o	book	book	o	o	o	o	o	book	book	o	o
take	o	o	book	book	o	o	o	o	o	book	book	o	o
turn	bell	o	o	o	o	o	o	o	o	o	o	o	bell

56

RULES OF THE GAME:

A phrasal verb is a verb with one (or two) prepositions or adverbs placed after it.
The effect is to obtain new verb meanings.

OBJECT OF THE GAME:

1) to practise the phrasal verbs beginning with the roots written vertically on the board.
2) to be the first player to reach the opposite side of the board from where you start.

REQUIREMENTS:

- from 2 to 4 players (or teams) (it is possible to practise alone)
- 1 die ⚁

SETTING UP THE BOARD AND PLAYERS:

First, it is necessary to choose 13 prepositions or adverbs from the list in the box at the top of the page and **write them randomly along the top row of the board**. This will ensure a different game each time you play.

Next, throw the die to decide Player 1, Player 2 etc. (Player 1 goes first, then Player 2 etc.)

Players (or teams) are represented by different coloured counters which are placed in the Player's Starting Boxes on the sidelines of the board.

HOW TO PLAY:

Moves are made according to the throw of the die and can be made in any direction, but you may not step on a square twice with the same throw.

STOPPING ON A SQUARE:

When you stop on a square, you must decide if the combination of root stem (horizontal column) and preposition or adverb (vertical column) is a valid English phrasal verb.

- If you can construct an accurate English sentence containing the phrasal verb, you may have another throw of the die.

- If your sentence is incorrect, however, you miss a turn.

- Note that your sentence should, if possible, help to explain the particular meaning of that phrasal verb.

- Note also that the phrasal verb may be transitive or intransitive.
    i.e. *look after (someone/something)* (transitive) and *look out* (intransitive)

- In addition, the sentence and phrasal verb may be in any tense you choose.

PLAYERS CAN CHECK WITH THE PHRASAL VERB KEY ON PAGE 58.

SPECIAL SQUARES: BELL, BOOK and CANDLE: 🔔 📖 🕯

Each player must obtain at least **one bell, one book and one candle** before arriving at the other side of the board. If you land on one of these squares and can correctly construct a sentence with the indicated phrasal verb, you obtain that symbol and may use it to cancel a missed turn in the future. A cancelled missed turn means you no longer 'own' that symbol and must obtain another before arriving at the other side of the board. Any number of symbols can be obtained.

ARRIVING AT THE OTHER SIDE OF THE BOARD:

You can arrive at any point on the other side of the board with any throw of the die BUT YOU MUST HAVE AT LEAST ONE BELL, ONE BOOK AND ONE CANDLE.

The other player(s) must then ask you to make a sentence using a **three part phrasal verb** of their choice such as *'put up with.'* (Check the 3-part Phrasal Verb Key for possible combinations.)

If you can correctly construct a sentence, you have WON THE GAME. If not, you must return to the square you were occupying before you threw the die and miss a turn.

PHRASAL VERB KEY:

For further information consult a reliable phrasal verb dictionary.
(See the Further Reading List on page 128.)

2-PART PHRASAL VERBS:

	about	across	against	apart	around	at	away	back	by	down	for	forward	in	into	off	on	out	over	round	through	to	up	with
be	◆		◆	◆	◆	◆	●	●		c	●	◆	+3 ●	c	●	●	+3 ●	●	◆	+3 c	●	+3 ●	◆
break	●	◆	◆	●	◆	●	+3 ●	c	●	●			+3 ●	●	●	●	+3 ●	●	◆	●	●	+3 ●	●
bring	●	◆	●	◆	●	●	●	●	●	●	●		●	◆	c	●	+3 ●	◆	●	●	◆	●	◆
come	●	●	●	●	●	●	+3 ●	●	c	+3 ●	◆	+3 ●	+3 ●	+3 ●	+3 ●	●	+3 ●	●	●	●	◆	+3 ●	●
get	●	◆	●	●	●	●	+3 ●	+3 ●	+3 ●	+3 ●			●	●	●	+3 ●	+3 ●	●	+3 ●	+3 ●	◆	+3 ●	◆
go	●	●	●	●	+3 ●	+3 ●	●	+3 ●	●	+3 ●	●	◆	+3 ◆	●	+3 ●	+3 ●	+3 ●	●	+3 ●	+3 ●	●	●	●
look	◆	●	◆		●	●	●	+3 ●	●	+3 ●	●	+3 ●	+3 ●	●	◆		+3 ●	●	◆	●	●	+3 ●	●
make		●	●	●			=3	●	●	●	●			●	+3 ●		●	c	◆		◆	+3 ●	◆
put	◆	●		●	●	●	●	●	●	+3 ●	●		+3 ●	●	●	●	●	●	●	●	◆	+3 ●	●
see	●	◆	●	●	●	◆	●	●		●	◆		●	●	●	●	●	●	●	●	●	●	●
set	●	●	●	●	●	●	◆	●	●	●	◆		●	◆	●	●	●	●	●	●	●	●	●
take	◆	●	●	●	●	●	●	●	●	●	●	+3 ●	+3 ●	●	●	●	+3 ●	+3 ●	●		◆	●	◆
turn	◆	●	●	●	●	●	+3 ●	●	●	●	●	●	●	●	●	●	●	●	●		●	●	◆

Key:

- ● a valid phrasal combination with a particular meaning
- c (usually) used only in colloquial speech
- +3 also used in a 3-part combination (see 3-PART PHRASAL VERBS)
- ◆ not a phrasal combination (although the words may go together)
- =3 only a 3-part combination is possible

3-PART PHRASAL VERBS:

be in for / be in on // be out of // be through with // be up to / be up against

break away from // break in on // break out in / break out of // break up with

bring out in / bring out (of*)

come away with // come down with / come down on // come forward with // come in for // come into use // come off it! // come out in / come out with // come up with / come up to / come up against

get away with // get back at // get by (with/on*) // get down to // get on with // get out of // get round to // get through to // get up to

go around (to*) / go around with // go back on // go down on / go down with // go in for // go off at // go on about / go on with / go through with

look back on // look down on // look forward to // look in on // look out for / look out of // look up to

make away with // make off with // make up for

put down to // put in for // put up with

take in (for*) // take (it) out on // take over from

turn away (from*) // turn up (with*)

* these prepositions do not constitute a seperate phrasal verb meaning, but often follow the two part phrasal verb

✪ VOCABULARY EXERCISES 3.1 - 3.3

3.1 WORD FORMATION: Complete the chart to provide the correct form of the words shown for the given parts of speech: (Not all forms are possible.)

NOUNS			ADJECTIVE	VERB	ADVERB
PLACE *	PERSON	GERUND/THING			
-	technician			-	
-			manufactured		-
-				compute	-
network					-
-	-	television			-
-	inventor				-
-				discover	-
-		import			-
-	-			-	effectively
construction					
-	-			evolve	-

* double word nouns are possible

3.2 PREFIXES (1): Note the meanings of the 9 prefixes given in the box below. Then work out the approximate meaning of the words that follow before checking their meanings in a good dictionary:

over = too much		**co** = together	**en** = make
under = too little	**il, in, im, ir, un** = not		

overdose ....
overshadow ....
underprivileged ....
cohabit ....
enlarge ....
illiterate ....
immeasurable ....
uncompromising ....

3.3 PREFIXES (2): Can you think of three more words beginning with each of the prefixes listed in the exercise above?

(ANSWERS ON PAGE 118)

◼️◼️ LISTENING EXERCISES 4.1 - 4.9

4.1 SPEED LISTENING: Note only the essential details of what you hear: (Refer to the tapescript for confirmation.)

a. London is ....

b. The Romans ....

c. The city ....

d. London ....

e. The Houses ....

f. The City ....

g. Most ....

h. ....

i. ....

j. ....

4.2 NUMBERS AND LETTERS: (Refer to the tapescript for confirmation.)

A i. .... ii. .... iii. .... iv. .... v. ....

vi. .... vii. .... viii. .... ix. .... x. ....

B i. .... ii. .... iii. .... iv. ....

v. .... vi. .... vii. .... viii. ....

ix. .... x. ....

C i. .... ii. .... iii. .... iv. ....

v. .... vi. .... vii. .... viii. ....

ix. .... x. ....

D i. .... ii. .... iii. .... iv. .... v. ....

vi. .... vii. .... viii. .... ix. .... x. ....

4.3 GENERAL INFORMATION: Listen to Radio Item 7 and complete the chart with the basic details: (Refer to the tapescript for confirmation.)

	What?	Where?	When?	Who?	How?	Why?
Radio Item 7						

4.4 GAPFILL:
Listen to Radio Item 7 a second time and complete the gaps in the summary of the passage below with the correct word or phrase you hear:

Research by linguists from a top (1)............... has resulted in a call for an increase in funding for English language training programmes. The research indicates that in certain (2)............... areas of Britain, (3)............... is no longer the dominant language. Mr. David Thorpe, a government representative, denies that there is a lack of (4)............... for English language programmes and has stated on radio that the reason for immigrants taking (5)............... to learn English is that there has been a slight (6)............... age shift in new migrants to city areas, and it is more difficult for (7)............... people people to learn a language. Obviously, English will remain the main language in (8)............... because the number of immigrants is only (9)............... every year. Enquiries for English language courses can be made by telephoning: (10)..................... .

4.5 SPECIFIC INFORMATION:
Listen again to Radio Item 7:

RADIO ITEM 7

   i.   According to the announcer, what has happened on a large scale in Britain since the 1950s?

   ii.   What has recent university research called into question?

   iii.   Who misrepresented the work conducted by a group of university linguists?

   iv.   According to Mr. Thorpe, what has happened to funding for English language training programmes?

   v.   What two reasons does Thorpe give to dismiss the suggestion that English will ever become a second language in Britain?

4.6 STATISTICS:
Study the diagrams below before listening to Radio Item 8. Then choose the diagram that describes the situation you hear on the tape:

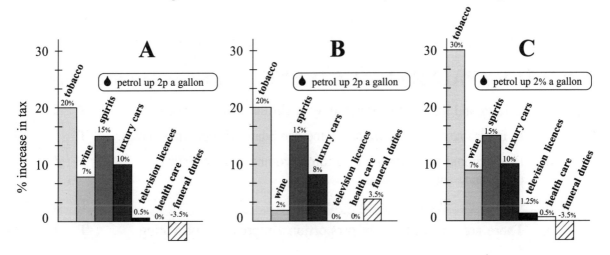

Now listen to Radio Item 8 again in detail and answer the following questions:

RADIO ITEM 8

   i.   When will the full tax increase be applied to luxury cars?

   ii.   Why is the government increasing the cost of a television licence?

   iii.   Which manufacturers of alcoholic beverages are not to be taxed?

   iv.   How is the government going to pay for its increased spending in health care?

4.7 DICTATION PREPARATION:

Look at the following words and phrases taken in sequence from the dictation in Exercise 4.8:

Democracy → three principles → representation → voting rights → minority views → tolerated → developed nations → economic success → democratic foundations → fair government → stability → prosperity → Nevertheless → government → arguing → issue → rather than → producing → result.

What is the likely main idea behind the dictation text?

Use the dictation practice in the following exercise (Exercise 4.8) to practise moving on to the next phrase spoken, even if you missed the previous phrase.

Pay particular attention to listening for the little words (articles, prepositions etc.) which are so easy to miss when taking down a dictation. Also, make sure your work is punctuated correctly.

4.8 DICTATION: Refer to Dictation 2 on the tape:

....

....

....

....

....

....

....

....

....

....

(Check your words, spelling and punctuation with the tapescript on page 107.)

4.9 TRUE / FALSE / NOT GIVEN: Listen to Lecture 4 on the tape:

a.	Britain and the United States have a similar voting system.	T	F	NG
b.	In British elections the winner is the candidate with the most votes.	T	F	NG
c.	Proportional representation requires voters to state their preference for candidates.	T	F	NG
d.	In Britain, all people must vote.	T	F	NG
e.	There are 2 main types of proportional representation voting systems.	T	F	NG
f.	France has a system of proportional representation.	T	F	NG
g.	Germany has an old-fashioned voting system.	T	F	NG
h.	Italy has a small number of political parties.	T	F	NG
i.	Proportional representation requires voters to be well-informed.	T	F	NG
j.	The lecturer is in favour of compulsory voting.	T	F	NG

(ANSWERS ON PAGE 119)

READING EXERCISES 4.1 - 4.11

☺ **4.1 PREDICTION:** Look at the illustration below and the words and phrases taken from the Reading Passage on the next page. With a partner if possible, try to predict exactly what is being discussed:

welfare societies   two major choices

government spending   strong connections with the unions

political scene   socialist

policies

fair division of wealth   environmental issues

the Conservative Party   the Labour Party

British voters   freedom

election   conservative, moderate and radical

less attention is paid to the smaller political parties

☺ **4.2 PRE-READING QUESTIONS:** Before reading the text on the following page, work with a partner and ask and answer the questions below. Base your answers on your possible knowledge of the topic:

❏ What system of government do you have in your country? (democratic? good? bad?)

❏ Is the party in power in your country conservative, radical, left, or socialist?

❏ How often are elections held in your country?

❏ What do you know about the system of government in your host country?

❏ Do you know the names of the 2 major political parties in Britain?

❏ What are the differences between the principles and policies held by the 2 major parties?

Now, supply the missing first and third letters in the mystery questions below:

1. -h-ch -o-itical -a-ty -n -r-tain (-n- -u-ope) -s -o-cerned -i-h -n-ironmental -s-ues?

   ....

2. -o -o- -n-w -h- -a-es -f -t-er -a-ties -n -h- -o-ntry -n -h-ch -o- -r- -t-dying?

   ....

4.3 SKIMMING: Read the text once for the gist (overall idea) and then in detail:

1 The British political scene is dominated by two major parties that have quite different political agendas. However, the ideological distance between the Labour Party and the Conservative Party has become less marked, and their policies more difficult to tell apart in recent years. In fact, it would be true to say that both parties consist of conservative,
5 moderate and radical elements, and therefore the general public is often perplexed about which party to vote for. Nonetheless, it is usual to find that a British voter will lean towards supporting one of these two parties and remain faithful to that party for life.

The Labour Party's manifest objective is to safeguard the interests of the common working man and woman, and, in effect, give them political representation in Parliament.
10 The Party has always had strong connections with the trade unions, and, before coming to power, was passionately committed to the concept of a welfare society in which people who are less fortunate than others are politically and financially assisted in their quest for a more equitable slice of the economic pie. The main problem is that such socialist agendas are extremely expensive to implement and maintain, even in a comparatively
15 wealthy country with a large working and, hence, taxpaying population base. Welfare societies tend towards bankruptcy unless government spending is kept in check. Fortunately, the present government recognises this, and has resisted reckless spending.

The Conservative Party, on the other hand, argues that the best way to ensure a fair division of wealth in the country is to allow more freedom to create it. This, in turn, means
20 more opportunities, jobs created etc., and therefore more wealth available to all. Just how the poor are to share in the distribution of this wealth (beyond being given, at least in theory, the opportunity to create it) is, however, less well understood. Practice, of course, may make nonsense of even the best theoretical intentions, and often the less politically powerful are badly catered for under governments implementing 'free-for-all' policies.

25 It is surprising, given the current homogeneity of the two major parties, that less attention than elsewhere in Europe is paid to the smaller political parties such as the Greens and the Liberal Democrats. This may be because British voters distrust parties with platforms based around one or two major current issues alone; the Green Party, for example, is almost solely concerned with the environment. Moreover, when it comes to casting a vote, history
30 shows that the British public tends to resist change and, thus, the status quo is maintained.

4.4 WORD DEFINITIONS: Find the single words in paragraphs 1 and 2 which mean the following:

i.	controlled or influenced (by)	v.	loyal ....
ii.	lists of things to be done	vi.	by comparison ....
iii.	(to) make safe	vii.	(to) put into practice.................
iv.	puzzled, confused	viii.	equal ....

4.5 TEXT ANALYSIS:

i. Which is the best title for the passage in Exercise 4.3?

  a) The Labour and Conservative Parties   c) Who the Public Should Vote For

  b) British Politics - an Overview   d) A Short History of Politics in Britain

ii. What is the main point of the first paragraph?

   a) British voters are confused about which political party to vote for

   c) Two political parties dominate the British political scene

   b) The policies of the two major British political parties are often similar

   d) The policies of the two major British parties differ greatly

iii. Which is the topic sentence of the second paragraph?

   a) Sentence number one

   c) The last sentence

   b) Sentence number two

   d) none of the above

iv. What is the main topic of the final paragraph of the passage?

   a) current political issues

   c) Attitudes of British voters

   b) The Green Party

   d) The smaller political parties

v. To what do the following pronouns in the passage refer?

   a) that *(line 7)* ....

   c) it *(line 22)* ....

   b) it *(line 18)* ....

   d) this *(line 27)* ....

4.6 GAPFILL:
The following is a summary of the passage in Exercise 4.3. Choose words/phrases from the box below and refer to the passage to fill the gaps:

Two parties (1)............... the British political scene: the Labour Party and the Conservative Party. Although (2)............... there are many similarities to be seen in their policies, British voters tend to stay (3)............... for life to the party of their choice. The (4)............... Party, encouraged by the (5)..............., supports a welfare-based (6)..............., whereas the (7)............... Party believes that (8)............... to pursue the creation of wealth ensures that all will eventually benefit from the opportunities created. Oddly, Britons do not follow Europeans by paying much (9)............... to smaller political parties, perhaps because their policies are based on just a few (10)............... political issues.

supporters	loyal	voters	support	recently	now
opportunities	Green	now	policies	freedom	Labour
politicians	control	attention	unions	money	leaning
Conservative	welfare	current	general public	majority	society

4.7 WORDS & PHRASES WITH SIMILAR MEANINGS:
Refer to the passage in Exercise 4.3, and see page 126 for advice on recognising pattern types. Circle the appropriate pattern type in each case.

i. distinguish between   → *(para. 1)* ....   (Pattern Type: **1 2 3**)

ii. tend towards   → *(para. 1)* ....   (Pattern Type: **1 2 3**)

iii. strong links with   → *(para. 2)* ....   (Pattern Type: **1 2 3**)

iv. population base   → *(para. 2)* ....   (Pattern Type: **1 2 3**)

v. the idea of	→ *(para. 2)*	(Pattern Type: **1 2 3**)
vi. helped to achieve	→ *(para. 2)*	(Pattern Type: **1 2 3**)
vii. monitored and limited	→ *(para. 2)*	(Pattern Type: **1 2 3**)

4.8 MATCHING SENTENCE HALVES: Refer to the text in Exercise 4.3 and match the halves of the given sentences together:

a. Labour and Conservative Party policies ...   + ...

b. The two major political parties are composed of ...   + ...

c. A large number of working individuals ...   + ...

d. The Conservative Party believes that ...   + ...

e. Government spending is likely to ...   + ...

f. A more equal share of the nation's wealth is unlikely to ...   + ...

g. ... mean bankruptcy in recent years.

h. ... the poor will become less politically powerful.

i. ... are becoming more difficult to distinguish between.

j. ... means more tax can be collected to support the disadvantaged.

k. ... the disadvantaged will benefit from an increase in the country's wealth.

l. ... conservative, moderate and radical groups of politicians.

m. ... increase under policies that encourage a welfare society.

n. ... occur under policies described as 'free-for-all'.

o. ... can afford to pay tax.

p. ... ensure a fair division of wealth under a Conservative Government.

4.9 TRUE / FALSE / NOT GIVEN: Refer to the text in Exercise 4.3.

a. Policies in support of the concept of a welfare society are costly.   **T   F   NG**

b. Britons usually vote for the party they supported early in life.   **T   F   NG**

c. The Labour Party was formed by the trade unions.   **T   F   NG**

d. Radical groups are only found within the Labour Party.   **T   F   NG**

e. The Conservative Party was formed after the Labour Party.   **T   F   NG**

f. Welfare-based societies invariably become bankrupt.   **T   F   NG**

g. According to the author, theories do not always work in practice.   **T   F   NG**

h. Some British voters are confused about who to vote for.   **T   F   NG**

i. The Green Parties are a lot smaller in European countries.   **T   F   NG**

j. The smaller parties are only concerned about the environment.   **T   F   NG**

4.10 SHORT-ANSWER QUESTIONS: Refer to the text in Exercise 4.3.

    i. Name the two groups whose interests the Labour Party looks after:

        1. ....

        2. ....

    ii. Why are socialist policies more costly in countries with a small working population?

        ....

    iii. What must governments limit to safeguard welfare societies from bankruptcy?

        ....

    iv. According to the author, who suffers under policies designed solely to create wealth?

        ....

    v. What do the smaller political parties' focus on?

        ....

    vi. How many political parties are named in the reading passage?

        ....

4.11 WORDSEARCH:
All words are taken from the Part 4 Listening and Reading Passages. Match the words and meanings in boxes A and B on the left. Next, locate the words in the wordsearch grid. (Answers to the clues are upside down and back-to-front under the grid - hold them up to a mirror):

A
1. "to pay ---------" (n) ..e..
2. foundation (n) ......
3. money, riches, large possessions (n) ......
4. faithful (adj) ......
5. search (n) ......
6. liberty, independence (n) ......

    a. (E L A W H T)
    b. (E T U Q S)
    c. (L L Y O A)
    d. (A E S B)
    e. (T O I N E T A N T)
    f. (M E R E F O D)

B
7. business, skilled craft (n/v) ......
8. those born overseas who live permanently abroad (n)......
9. of a central system of government (adj) ......
10. alone, accompanied (adv) ......
11. completely controlled (adj) ......
12. fictitious thing or idea (n) ......

    g. (O I E A M D D N T)
    h. (G T S A I M R N)
    i. (Y L L O S E)
    j. (T D E A R)
    k. (T M H Y)
    l. (E A E D L R F)

D	H	L	A	Y	O	L	S	N
V	E	T	X	C	T	T	O	P
M	L	T	L	R	N	I	L	G
B	O	A	A	A	T	M	E	T
A	P	D	R	N	E	N	L	M
S	E	G	E	E	I	W	Y	Y
E	I	T	X	E	D	M	M	T
M	T	Z	U	J	R	E	O	H
A	T	S	E	U	Q	F	F	D

6. FREEDOM   12. MYTH
5. QUEST   11. DOMINATED
4. LOYAL   10. SOLELY
3. WEALTH   9. FEDERAL
2. BASE   8. MIGRANTS
1. ATTENTION   7. TRADE

(Hold up to a mirror to view answers!)

(ANSWERS ON PAGE 119)

✍ WRITING EXERCISES 4.1 - 4.7

4.1 IDENTIFYING THE MAIN FEATURES: Writing Task 1:

Identify 8 key features of the information given in the graph for the TWO companies Acme Sports Cars and Branson Motors. (Note that you are not asked to include information about Curtis Car Mart.) Then complete the sentences below the graph.

The graph below shows the monthly profits of 3 British companies in the car retail industry for the 2000 financial year.

Write a report for a university lecturer comparing the performance of Acme Sports Cars and Branson Motors for the period given.

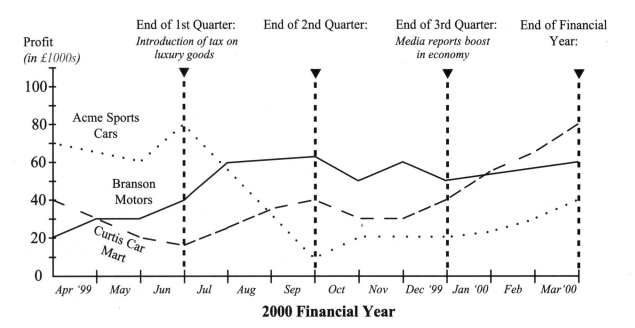

MAIN FEATURES:

1. ...*Acme Sports Cars*...... monthly profit began higher than that of ....

2. By the end of the financial year .... monthly profit was three times what it was at the beginning of the year ...

3. ... whereas the monthly profit of .... had almost halved.

4. The worst quarter for Acme Sports Cars was from .... to ....

5. The best two months for Branson Motors were .... and ....

6. The profit situation for Branson Motors fluctuated between .... and ....

7. The introduction of the luxury goods tax badly affected ....

8. The monthly profit of Acme Sports Cars peaked at ....

4.2 SENTENCE INSERTION: Practice for Writing Task 1:

Insert the statistical information from the graph in Exercise 4.1 into the blank spaces in the model answer on the following page and in the 'missing sentences' labelled 'a' to 'd'. Then complete the answer by inserting the 'missing' sentences, and finally, add the verb and adverb phrases in the shaded spaces A - D.

WRITING TASK 1 - Model Answer:

para.1 **(i)** .... The former was making almost twice the profit at the beginning than at the end of the financial year. **(ii)**.................................... .

para.2 During the first quarter, Acme Sports Cars' monthly profit (A)......................... from (1)_____ to (2)_____ , but (B).................... to (3)_____ by the end of June. **(iii)**.. .

para.3 Due to the introduction of a luxury goods tax, Acme Sports Cars' monthly profit (C)........................ during the second quarter from (4)_____ to only (5)_____ , whereas that of Branson Motors continued to rise, peaking at just over (6)_____ by the end of September.

para.4 **(iv)**... . At the beginning of the last quarter, a boost in the economy meant the monthly profit of both Acme Sports Cars and Branson Motors (D)......................... to (7)_____ and (8)_____ respectively by the financial year's end.

fell dramatically	gradually increased	decreased slightly	rose sharply

a. In the third quarter, Acme Sports Cars' monthly profit increased steadily to (9)_____ and remained stable, while Branson Motors' monthly profits fluctuated between just over (10)_____ and (11)_____ .

b. Branson Motors' monthly profit, however, doubled from (12)_____ to (13)_____ .

c. The graph shows the four quarters of the (14)_____ financial year and the monthly profit of Acme Sports Cars and Branson Motors for (15)_____ months.

d. There was a three-fold increase in the latter's monthly profit over the same period.

4.3 THE TOPIC & THE TOPIC QUESTION: Writing Task 2:

Circle the topic and write the topic question as a 'wh' or yes/no question:

Example: **'Although abuses of the system are inevitable, (social welfare payments) are essential to protect the rights citizens have to a guaranteed minimum income in a democratic society.' Discuss.**
Are (they) essential to protect citizens' rights to a guaranteed income?

a. The government is ultimately responsible for making the streets safe. Stronger gun laws should be in force to protect all citizens. How far do you agree or disagree with this statement?

    ....

b. The only way to reduce the rising number of road accidents is for a total ban on drinking while driving. Do you agree or disagree? Make other recommendations.

    ....

c. Most British people believe they enjoy and have the right to free speech. How important is it to have the right to say or write whatever you wish in society?

    ....

4.4 BRAINSTORMING: There are four essay tasks mentioned in Exercise 4.3. The 21 arguments listed below belong to four essays written as answers to those tasks. Complete the following table by first deciding **which argument** belongs to which essay, and second, if each argument is **for** or **against** the topic question.

The example essay columns have been completed for you:

EXAMPLE ESSAY		ESSAY a.		ESSAY b.		ESSAY c.	
For	Against	For	Against	For	Against	For	Against
2	8	....	....	....	....	....	....
14	16	....	....	....	....	....	....
21	....	....	....	....	....	....	....

1. Crime is on the increase in cities, and the percentage of robberies in which arms are used is rising, too.

2. Not all those people who receive social welfare payments are able or capable of earning a wage. They have a right to an income, too.

3. A reduction in gun ownership would only occur if there were enough police to enforce the stronger laws.

4. A democracy can only be strong and healthy if it allows people with radical opinions to say what they wish. Words never hurt anyone.

5. Why only ban alcohol? There are many other drugs which impair one's ability to drive. The complete ban of only one substance makes no sense.

6. Guns kill. Since we cannot prohibit their manufacture we must have effective, that is, stronger gun laws.

7. We are not free to do whatever else we like, so why should we believe we have the right to free speech?

8. People should look after themselves. Welfare increases dependency on others and destroys dignity.

9. Almost anyone can buy a gun if they can provide proof of the need to own one. It is too easy to buy a gun.

10. Tests prove that most car accidents occur as a result of speeding. Drivers still speed even when they have not been drinking alcohol. Targeting alcohol does not stop people speeding.

11. The only way to prevent crime is to reduce the need for crime, that is, to reduce poverty. Gun ownership makes no difference.

12. The only persons against a total ban are the manufacturers of alcoholic drinks and pub owners. Unfortunately, these two groups are politically influential and wealthy. Most others support it.

13. The best way to make a better world is to prevent certain people from expressing their opinions. This means censoring what they say so that others do not become influenced.

14. Crime increases if people have no means of support. It is cheaper to pay welfare than police the streets.

15. In countries where it is illegal to drink and drive, the road death toll is far less than in countries which allow alcohol in the bloodstream while driving.

16. If you have no job, you should not expect the government to help you. It is your family's responsibility.

17. People who oppose free speech are only afraid that what they believe may not be the truth. Many great ideas of the past were first banned from being heard.

18. Since speeding is the leading cause of accidents, and alcohol makes people less careful and more likely to speed, it makes sense to totally ban drinking while driving.

19. Banning people from saying what they wish only makes them try harder to be heard.

20. It would be better if guns were not manufactured. However, they are needed in the military, on the farm and for sporting purposes. Stronger laws have little or no effect, since criminals can always buy guns.

21. People who pay taxes all their working lives have the right to an income if they lose their jobs, especially if it is not their own fault.

Next, for each essay, decide which is the **easiest** side of the argument to defend (**for** or **against**). Is it because there are more arguments, or are they easier to express?

4.5 PLANNING: A university tutor has asked you to write the following essay:

'Although abuses of the system are inevitable, social welfare payments are essential to protect the rights of citizens to a guaranteed minimum income in a modern society.' Discuss.

Complete the plan below with ideas of your own or from Exercise 4.4. Then check with the model answer and plan in the Answer Key on page 120.

PLAN

TOPIC: Social welfare payments

TYPE 'A' QUESTION * :   Are (they) essential to protect our rights to a guaranteed income?

INTRO: General statement + acknowledgement of system abuse
(at least 40 words)   BUT: my opinion → YES, essential
                                            for 2 MAIN REASONS: 1. ....
                                                            2. ...*Many require welfare*....

BODY:

PARAGRAPH 1: (YES + WHY)   REASON 1: ....
(at least 60 words)   ARGUMENT 1: ....
                                            ....
                    Example/s: (?)   ....
                                            ....
ARGUMENT 2:   Example/s: (?) ....

PARAGRAPH 2: (YES + WHY)   REASON 2: ....
(at least 60 words)   ARGUMENT 1:
                                            ....
                    Example/s: (?)   ....
                                            ARGUMENT 2: ....
                    Example/s: (?)   ....

PARAGRAPH 3: (NO)   REASON 1: ....
(at least 60 words)   ....
                    Refutation: ....
                                            ....
                                            REASON 2: ....
                                            ....
                    Refutation: ....
                                            ....

CONCLUSION: *(YES + SUMMARY)* → WHAT IS PROVED: ....
(at least 30 words)   ....
                    Summary point: ....

---

* TYPE 'A' QUESTIONS require an **argument** essay. For more information refer to pages 64 and 65 of *'101 Helpful Hints for IELTS'*.

(ANSWERS ON PAGES 119 - 120)

?! PUNCTUATION EXERCISES 4.1 - 4.2

4.1 PUNCTUATION MARKS: Match the following punctuation marks, their names, and their uses:

SYMBOL		NAME	WHEN USED
(i)	:	a) comma	1. at the end of a sentence
(ii)	' '	b) full stop	2. to separate parts of a sentence and around most linking words
(iii)	?	c) colon	3. to separate sub-groups within lists, and to join two independent, grammatically complete and related clauses
(iv)	!	d) semi-colon	4. to draw attention to what is to follow
(v)	,	e) parentheses	5. for quotes and titles *
(vi)	( )	f) apostrophe	6. to show possession or contraction
(vii)	;	g) question mark	7. to emphasise, but avoid use in a formal writing
(viii)	.	h) quotation marks	8. to include additional but non-essential information
(ix)	'	i) exclamation mark	9. to indicate a sentence is interrogative (in question form)

* double quotation marks (" ") are also used, but are less common in formal assignment writing since referencing is more usual. However, the IELTS test does not require references.

4.2 PUNCTUATION: Place the correct punctuation marks at the points illustrated within the following texts taken from Reading Passage 4:

A the british political scene is dominated by two major parties that have quite different political agendas however the ideological distance between the labour party and the conservative party has become less marked and their policies more difficult to tell apart in recent years in fact it would be true to say that both parties consist of conservative moderate and radical elements and therefore the general public is often perplexed about which party to vote for nonetheless it is usual to find that a british voter will lean towards supporting one of these two parties and remain faithful to that party for life

B the conservative party on the other hand argues that the best way to ensure a fair division of wealth in the country is to allow more freedom to create it this in turn means more opportunities jobs created etc and therefore more wealth available to all just how the poor are to share in the distribution of this wealth beyond being given at least in theory the opportunity to create it is however less well understood practice of course may make nonsense of even the best theoretical intentions and often the less politically powerful are badly catered for under governments implementing free-for-all policies

(ANSWERS ON PAGE 121)

❋ SPELLING EXERCISES 4.1 - 4.2

4.1 SPELLING ERRORS: All the following sentences contain spelling errors. First, find all the incorrectly spelt words. Next, **rank the sentences** in order according to the number of errors they contain (from 1 to 12 errors):

a. It is a pitty that politishians are so often abussed when politics is, in fact, a noble proffession.

b. Howevver, there are few nowble politicians; ruthlesness being allmost a prereckwisite theez daze.

c. Allso, it is a lot mor dificult now then in the passed to ryze to the top without havving an independant fortoone.

d. In addition, the temtation to give in to presure groups instead of pursueing a proper course of action is all too common.

e. The puplic has alwayz respectd stronng leders; the problm is tryeing two determin wat acktualy constitootes strength.

f. Is it considered a sign of strength to do all one can to ruin the reputation of an oponent?

g. Is strength stubborness in the face of overwelming opposition?

h. Obvously, the varst magority of electers believe that political strength is the ability to argue and scream instead of to debate, and to refuse to give in even when prooved wrong.

i. Sertainly, sellf-intrest is allmost the ownly critearion four choseing a politican to vote for on elecstion dae.

j. It is theirfore not suprising that self-interrested men and woman get ellected to offise.

k. Perrhaps we shoold not be too qwick too blaime those elekted to carrie owt our wishes.

l. In democrasies, peple invarably get the govenments they desserve, wich is a rather sad indictment off the inteligense of both the generral publik and our polticians.

RANKING: ....

4.2 CORRECT SPELLING?: Only some of the following words are spelt correctly. Circle those that are incorrect and spell them properly below:

qwalify   query   questionaire   recognise   referrence

....

regulate   rellated   rellevant   reserch   resource   revize

....

sammple   seminnar   sequence   spesialise   statistics   submit   sumarise

....

servey   sylabus   technalogical   tertiery   theoretical   theses   transffer

....

tuiton   tutourial   undergraduet   vallid   variaibles   vocaburary   vocational

....

(ANSWERS ON PAGE 121)

GRAMMAR EXERCISES 4.1 - 4.10

4.1 3RD PERSON SINGULAR AGREEMENT?: Check the verbs and their subjects in the following sentences, and make the agreement of the verb with the 3rd person singular subject where necessary:

a. The main purpose of government .... (be) to provide a stable framework of management, within which a country .... (grow) steadily and can .... (prosper).

b. Most people, however, usually .... (take) the view that deciding moral issues eventually .... (become) the governments' responsibility.

c. In other words, the government .... (be) not only responsible for managing the economy; it .... (decide) what a member of society can and cannot .... (do) within that society.

d. A democracy must .... (allow) freedom of thought and expression, but this .... (do) not mean that all ideas and actions can be tolerated; an individual or group of persons who intentionally .... (violate) democratic principles must be restrained.

e. The majority of people .... (believe) that governments should set and maintain the moral code within society, but when this .... (occur), personal freedom is put at risk and .... (lose) its perceived importance.

f. It is often difficult for a politician who .... (argue) the case for personal freedom when the general public .... (demand) a traditional approach to moral issues.

g. Politicians almost always .... (take) a pragmatic approach to their work. The ideal politician, however, ... (do) not easily compromise his or her principles.

4.2 SUBJECT AND VERB AGREEMENT: Match the sentence beginnings on the left with the correct endings on the right, and provide a suitable verb from the box below to join the two sentence halves together:

a. The Prime Minister ...

b. A more equitable society ...

c. One of the most problematical political issues of recent years, funding for the National Health Service, ...

d. Comprehensive schools ...

e. In modern day societies, banks ...

i. ... increasingly harder to achieve.

ii. ... recently at the hands of inept politicians too concerned with saving money.

iii. ... great control over the country's financial future.

iv. ... the present government.

v. ... a speech on taxation to Parliament.

| is becoming | has divided | have exerted | have suffered | has delivered |

a. ....

b. ....

c. ....

d. ....

e. ....

4.3 VERB + -ING or VERB + TO + INFINITIVE: Choose the words from the oval box that can form the construction in the boxes on the left. Note that some, but not all, words can form part of both constructions:

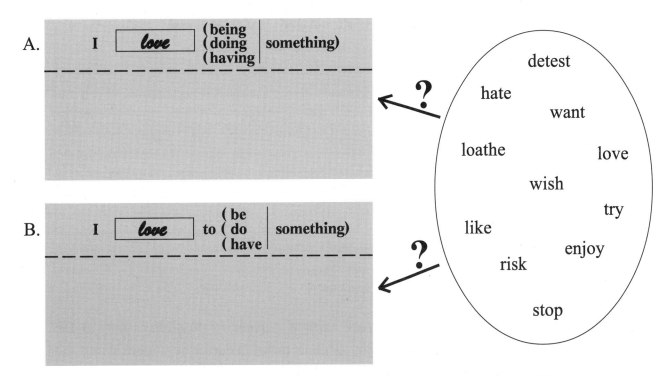

A. I | *love* | (being (doing   something) (having

B. I | *love* | to (be (do   something) (have

detest
hate
want
loathe   love
wish
try
like
risk   enjoy
stop

4.4 VERB + PREPOSITION + -ING or VERB + TO + INFINITIVE:
Choose the words from the oval box that can form the construction in the boxes on the left. Some, but not all, words can form part of both constructions:

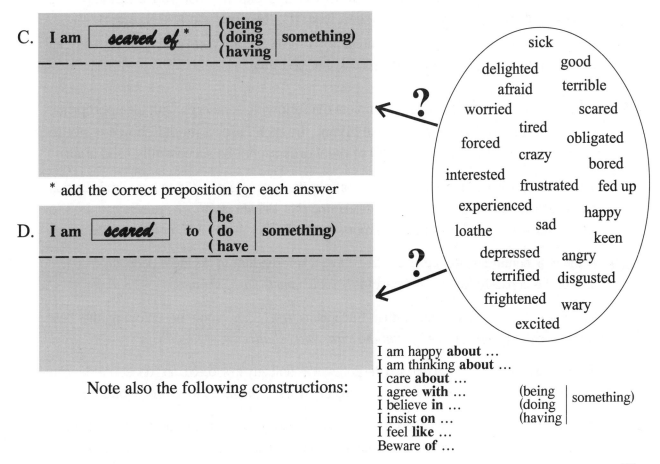

C. I am | *scared of* * | (being (doing   something) (having

* add the correct preposition for each answer

D. I am | *scared* | to (be (do   something) (have

Note also the following constructions:

sick
delighted   good
afraid   terrible
worried   scared
tired
forced   obligated
crazy   bored
interested   fed up
frustrated
experienced   happy
loathe   sad   keen
depressed   angry
terrified   disgusted
frightened   wary
excited

I am happy **about** …
I am thinking **about** …
I care **about** …
I agree **with** …   (being
I believe **in** …   (doing   something)
I insist **on** …   (having
I feel **like** …
Beware **of** …

4.5 MODAL VERBS (1): Complete the following chart with a tick (✓)
depending on whether the modal construction is possible or not:

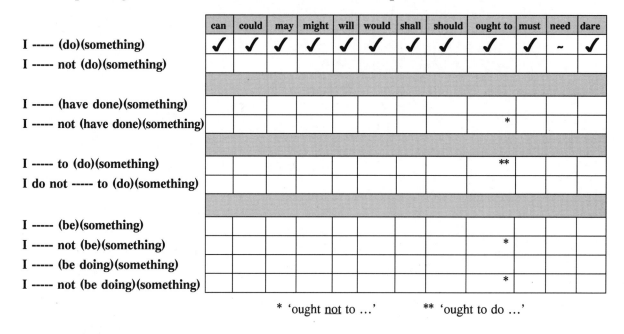

	can	could	may	might	will	would	shall	should	ought to	must	need	dare
I ----- (do)(something)	✓	✓	✓	✓	✓	✓	✓	✓	✓	✓	~	✓
I ----- not (do)(something)												
I ----- (have done)(something)												
I ----- not (have done)(something)									*			
I ----- to (do)(something)									**			
I do not ----- to (do)(something)												
I ----- (be)(something)												
I ----- not (be)(something)									*			
I ----- (be doing)(something)												
I ----- not (be doing)(something)									*			

* 'ought not to ...'   ** 'ought to do ...'

4.6 MODAL VERBS (2): Work with a partner if possible, refer to the
completed chart above and take it in turns to make accurate sentences using the
given modal verb constructions in Exercise 4.5:

e.g. "I **might** vote for the government candidate (... **if** ... she promises to reduce taxes.)"
"I **needn't** pay so much in tax this year (... **because** ... I earnt so little.)"

Try to complete your sentences with words that explain that you understand the
meaning of the modal verb construction (use 'if', 'because' etc.).

You might wish to choose a particular topic area for all your answers, or you can
choose a different topic for each answer that you give.

4.7 MODAL VERBS (3): Complete the following sentences with the appropriate
choice of a modal verb from those given. In each case, a modal choice is not to
be used more than once, and TWO of the words cannot be successfully used at all.

a. The latest government crisis (1)………. affect the outcome of talks today which British
dairy farmers are hoping (2)……….determine that Britain (3)………. not be required to
accept further reductions in dairy exports to the EEC. *(dare, will, could, should, must)*

b. If the war continues, do we (4)………. have a referendum to decide if people (5)……….
accept the conscription of 18 year olds? *(will, must, dare, should)*

c. There (6)………. be no doubt that Europeans (7)………. soon be enjoying the best
economical climate for years. *(might, can, will, shall)*

d. The minister (8)………. have realised the policy was unlikely to succeed, and done something to
rectify the situation before it (9)………. get any worse. *(oughtn't to, could, should, won't)*

e. We (10)………. have to wait and see if the election (11)………. change the way people feel,
but we (12)………. not expect too much too soon. *(will, shall, should, would, ought to)*

4.8 CLAUSES OF TIME: These come before or after the main clause. From the box, add the appropriate time clause (and a comma?) to the given main clauses:

> **since** the introduction of tighter tax laws   **while** voters considered their options
> **when** a politician is proved to be corrupt   **as soon as** the election results came in
> **before** voters go to the polling booth

a. it was clear that the public was unhappy with the previous government's performance

....

b.   both political parties were busy making even more election promises

....

c.   a government should fully disclose its policies

....

d.   there is usually an increase in accountability of all political representatives

....

e.   more money has become available to the government to implement its policies

....

4.9 CLAUSES OF CONTRAST: Join the following sentences together with the correct choice of linking word or phrase from those in the brackets:

a. The National Government is responsible for the nation's security. Local governments are responsible for administration at a much lower level. *(whereas* or *even though)*

b. The trading policies of most EEC countries are similar. They did not always share a a common goal. *(while* or *although)*

c. Politicians used to overlook the needs of immigrants to Britain. There was a need for improved English training programmes. *(despite* or *on the other hand)*

d. Major strikes cost the country enormous amounts of money. They are sometimes necessary to correct imbalances of power between employers and employees.
(on the contrary or *however)*

e. Social security benefits ensure that the disadvantaged do not suffer. Abuses of the system invariably occur. *(in spite of* or *but)*

Now practise using the linking words or phrases above in sentences of your own.

4.10 CLAUSES OF REASON AND PURPOSE: Make the best match of the main clauses on the left, and the clauses of reason and purpose below:

a. The democratic system, while flawed, must be protected at all costs ...

i. ... **because** certain major issues require compromise. *(reason)*

b. Our leaders sometimes have to introduce unpopular financial measures ...

ii. ... **since** it is necessary to combat discriminatory practices. *(reason)*

c. Political parties should work together to solve the nation's problems ...

iii. ... **to** protect local industries. *(purpose)*

d. Certain groups of people should relinquish their favoured status in society ...

iv. ... **in order to** raise revenue through taxation. *(purpose)*

e. In my opinion, the government should not introduce tariffs on imported goods ...

v. ... **so that** the will of the majority of the people is respected. *(purpose)*

(ANSWERS ON PAGES 121 - 122)

★ VOCABULARY EXERCISES 4.1 - 4.3

4.1 WORD FORMATION: Complete the chart to provide the correct form of the words shown for the given parts of speech: (Not all forms are possible.)

NOUNS			ADJECTIVE	VERB	ADVERB
PLACE *	PERSON	GERUND/THING			
-		politics			
-				govern	
department	-				-
	-		responsible	-	
	-	negotiator			
	-			meet	-
-	-			recommend	-
		system			
-					productively
-	economist				
		control			-

* double word nouns are possible

4.2 PREFIXES (1): Note the meanings of the 5 prefixes given in the box below. Then work out the approximate meaning of the words that follow before checking their meanings in a good dictionary:

inter	= between	**post**	= after
pre **fore**	= before	**re**	= again

interaction ....
interplanetary ....
prehistoric ....
foregoing ....
posthumous ....
reconsider ....
recolonise ....

4.3 PREFIXES (2): Can you think of three more words beginning with each of the prefixes listed in the exercise above?

(ANSWERS ON PAGE 122)

◢▱◣ **LISTENING EXERCISES 5.1 - 5.9**

5.1 SPEED LISTENING: Complete the table with the essential details of what you hear: (Refer to the tapescript for confirmation.)

UNIVERSITIES:	OXFORD	CAMBRIDGE
Location		
Population (city)		
When founded		
Undergraduates		
Famous alumni		
Women		
Colleges		
Tourists		

5.2 SEQUENCING: Put the following groups of 5 sentences in the correct order (1 to 5) according to the sequence in which they are given in Lecture 5:

...... Visitors notice the architecture and the climate.

..1... Heathrow International Airport is usually a visitor's first taste of England.

...... Students who are staying with an English family are met at the airport.

...... The city is approximately a £20 taxi fare from the airport.

...... Visitors quickly become aware that London is a busy city.

↘ ...... The first visit is to the English college chosen in the home country.

...... A visitor takes a few days to recover from the flight.

...... Trains are the preferred method of travel in and around the city.

..1... In London people usually do not live in completely separate houses

...... The language colleges are situated near tube stations.

↙ ...... Each new student to the college takes a class placement test.

...... Students hear information about the school and its programmes.

...... London has a great many international restaurants.

...... Some students bring their own lunch with them to the college.

..1... Students get together in the common room of the college.

↘ ..1... Teaching methods in an English-speaking country can be quite unexpected.

...... Students attend their first class of the course and meet their classmates.

...... At the end of the day it is usually agreed that leaving home was worth it.

...... Students are treated as adults.

...... Students exchange personal information in class.

5.3 TRUE / FALSE / NOT GIVEN: What do you remember from listening to Lecture 5? Answer the following questions before listening again:

a. Most visitors to England arrive at Heathrow International Airport. **T   F   NG**
b. Family houses in the city are usually only partly detached. **T   F   NG**
c. Family accommodation is more expensive than sharing with friends. **T   F   NG**
d. The English language college is chosen when you arrive in London. **T   F   NG**
e. The Underground train system is more expensive than the buses. **T   F   NG**
f. Students choose their programme on the first day of the course. **T   F   NG**
g. The price of food at restaurants in London is usually quite expensive. **T   F   NG**
h. During the first lesson, students find out about their classmates. **T   F   NG**

5.4 DICTATION: Refer to Dictation 3 on the tape:

....
....
....
....
....
....
....
....
....

(Check your words, spelling and punctuation with the tapescript on page 109.)

5.5 MULTIPLE CHOICE QUESTIONS (1): Listen to Conversation 1 and choose the correct answer to the following questions:

i. Before the IELTS test Erica:
   a) did not do any practice
   b) took a short practice course
   c) studied the library
   d) studied vocabulary

ii. The IELTS Writing Tasks were:
   a) 250 words long
   b) 2000 words long
   c) extremely hard according to Erica
   d) both to do with computers

iii. Erica's IELTS Listening Test was:
   a) slow enough to catch the words
   b) the most difficult Sub-test
   c) faster than Ilsa's Listening Test
   d) none of the above

iv. Erica's Speaking Test included:
   a) a 3 minute role play
   b) a role play about the weather
   c) a speech about her family
   d) questions about buses and trains

v. In 3 months Erica's overall Band Score:
   a) increased by one band
   b) should increase by one band
   c) will increase by one band
   d) will be the same as Ilsa's

5.6 MULTIPLE CHOICE QUESTIONS (2): Discover why each of the wrong answers in Exercise 5.5 is **incorrect**. (See page 126 for a list of reasons why possible answers to multiple choice questions can be incorrect.) You might want to do the same with the other multiple choice exercises in this book.

5.7 DIRECTIONS (1): Listen to Conversation 2, and follow the direction of the tour Linda will give her students on the map below:

As you listen, fill in the **missing names of the buildings** …

… and the **time** she must arrive at or leave each destination.

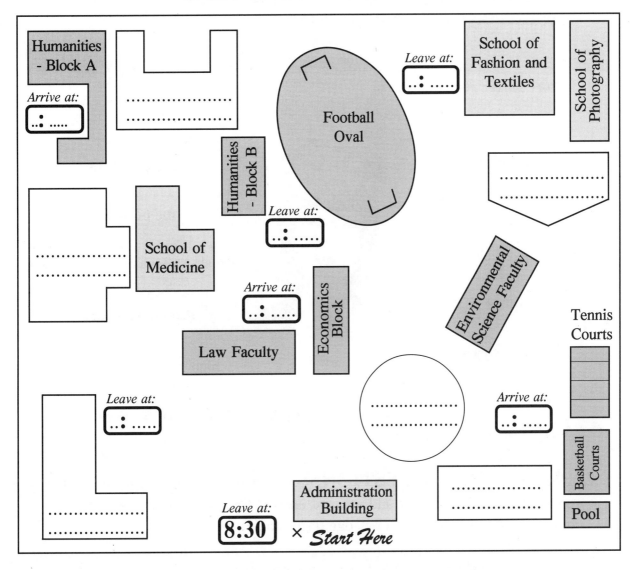

5.8 DIRECTIONS (2): Next, try to answer the following questions from memory before listening again to the conversation:

a. Which group of students will Ross show around the university? ....

b. In which direction will Ross take his students? ....

c. Why are the student photo sessions taking place in the Sports Centre this semester?

....

d. When can Linda show her students the Student Centre? ....

☺ **5.9 DIRECTIONS (3):** With a partner if possible, give the directions of the tour that **Ross** will give. Remember, he will go in the opposite direction to Linda.

(ANSWERS ON PAGE 123)

READING EXERCISES 5.1 - 5.11

☺ **5.1 PREDICTION:** Look at the illustration below and the words and phrases taken from the Reading Passage on the next page. With a partner if possible, try to predict exactly what is being discussed:

bias

competition is the driving force

future career requirements

universities

better educated

criticised as alarmist

extra workload

vast amounts of extra money

the push is universal

educational psychologist

Gatsby raises a number of issues

the workplace

drop in standards

earning capacity

high stress levels

social pressures

candidates without qualifications

☺ **5.2 PRE-READING QUESTIONS:** Before reading the text on the following page, work with a partner and ask and answer the questions below. Base your answers on your possible knowledge of the topic:

❏ What educational qualifications do you presently have?

❏ Do you intend to gain further academic qualifications? If so, why?

❏ How important is it to have good qualifications these days? Was it always so?

❏ Do you think studying should be for pleasure or simply as a means to get ahead in life?

❏ In your opinion, are employers too concerned with academic qualifications these days?

❏ If you were a boss, would you hire a person lacking suitable academic qualifications?

Now, supply the missing first and third letters in the mystery questions below:

1. -h-uld -m-loyees -e -e-uired -o -o-tinue -o -t-dy -n -r-er -o -e-p -h-ir -o-s?

   ....

2. -o -o- -h-nk -e-tiary -d-cation -h-uld -e -r-e?

   ....

5.3 SKIMMING: Read the text once for the gist (overall idea) and then in detail:

para 1. The need for a satisfactory education is more important than ever before. Nowadays, without a qualification from a reputable school or university, the odds of landing that plum job advertised in the paper are considerably shortened. Moreover, one's present level of education could fall well short of future career requirements.

para 2. It is no secret that competition is the driving force behind the need to obtain increasingly higher qualifications. In the majority of cases, the urge to upgrade is no longer the result of an insatiable thirst for knowledge. The pressure is coming from within the workplace to compete with ever more qualified job applicants, and in many occupations one must now battle with colleagues in the reshuffle for the position one already holds.

para 3. Striving to become better educated is hardly a new concept. Wealthy parents have always been willing to spend the vast amounts of extra money necessary to send their children to schools with a perceived educational edge. Working adults have long attended night schools and refresher courses. Competition for employment has been around since the curse of working for a living began. Is the present situation so very different to that of the past?

para 4. The difference now is that the push is universal and from without as well as within. A student at a comprehensive school receiving low grades is no longer as easily accepted by his or her peers as was once the case. Similarly, in the workplace, unless employees are engaged in part-time study, they may be frowned upon by their employers and peers and have difficulty even standing still. In fact, in these cases, the expectation is for careers to go backwards and earning capacity to take an appreciable nosedive.

para 5. At first glance, the situation would seem to be laudable; a positive response to the exhortations of politicians for us all to raise our intellectual standards and help improve the level of intelligence within the community. Yet there are serious ramifications according to at least one educational psychologist. Dr. Brendan Gatsby has caused some controversy in academic circles by suggesting that a bias towards what he terms 'paper excellence' might cause more problems than it is supposed to solve. Gatsby raises a number of issues that affect the individual as well as society in general.

para 6. Firstly, he believes the extra workload involved is resulting in abnormally high stress levels in both students at comprehensive schools and adults studying after working hours. Secondly, skills which might be more relevant to the undertaking of a sought-after job are being overlooked by employers not interviewing candidates without qualifications on paper. These two areas of concern for the individual are causing physical as well as emotional stress.

para 7. Gatsby also argues that there are attitudinal changes within society to the exalted role education now plays in determining how the spoils of working life are distributed. Individuals of all ages are being driven by social pressures to achieve academic success solely for monetary considerations instead of for the joy of enlightenment. There is the danger that some universities are becoming degree factories with an attendant drop in standards. Furthermore, our education system may be rewarding doggedness above creativity; the very thing tutors ought to be encouraging us to avoid. But the most undesirable effect of this academic paper chase, Gatsby says, is the disadvantage that 'user pays' higher education confers on the poor, who invariably lose out to the more financially favoured.

para 8. Naturally, although there is agreement that learning can cause stress, Gatsby's comments regarding university standards have been roundly criticised as alarmist by most educationists who point out that, by any standard of measurement, Britain's education system overall, at both secondary and tertiary levels, is equal to that of any in the world.

5.4 MATCHING HEADINGS (1): Match the headings on page 84 to the paragraphs in the text. The first paragraph has been done for you:

Paragraph 1. .....*d*......   Paragraph 5. ....

Paragraph 2. ....   Paragraph 6. ....

Paragraph 3. ....   Paragraph 7. ....

Paragraph 4. ....   Paragraph 8. ....

a. Causes of concern for the individual.

b. The struggle for better education results in parents sending children to costlier schools.

c. Doubts as to whether competition is a modern phenomenon.

d. The value of education in securing employment.

e. Questions raised concerning the over-emphasis placed on paper qualifications.

f. Reaction to criticism of perceived bias towards paper qualifications.

g. Social consequences of the push for further education.

h. Comprehensive school students no longer receive low grades.

i. Competition in the workplace increasing the need for higher qualifications.

j. Pressure to perform well at school and continue study while working.

k. Positive response to the urging of educationalists to increase learning.

l. Dr. Gatsby proves that learning causes stress.

m. The disadvantage of 'user pays' education systems.

5.5 MATCHING HEADINGS (2): Next, match the **5 wrong answers** above with the **3 reasons why they are incorrect** given below. Note that some reasons are used twice:

Answers

1. The (possible) answer is not the main idea of the paragraph but an example supporting the main idea. ....*b*..........

2. The (possible) answer is not a statement made in the text. ....

3. The (possible) answer is mentioned in the paragraph but the main point of the paragraph is an alternative viewpoint. ....

5.6 MATCHING DEFINITIONS: Match the left column words and phrases (taken from the text) with the meanings in the right column:

1) i. the odds are shortened   a. main push
   ii. plum job   b. not come close to the (desired) level
   iii. fall well short (of)   c. desire to increase the status (of)
   iv. driving force   d. highly desired job
   v. urge to upgrade   e. prejudice
   vi. bias   f. the chances are lessened

2) i. reshuffle   a. persons of equal rank or status
   ii. exalted role   b. workmates
   iii. perceived edge   c. noticeably large drop
   iv. peers   d. something has this when it is seen to be better
   v. colleagues   e. highly praised position
   vi. appreciable nosedive   f. a redistribution

3) i. serious ramifications   a. important consequences
   ii. academic circles   b. accompanying decline
   iii. sought-after job   c. profits from working
   iv. spoils of working life   d. a job lots of people want
   v. attendant drop   e. severely attack
   vi. roundly criticise   f. groups of academically qualified people

5.7 GAPFILL: The following is a summary of part of the passage in Exercise 5.3. Choose words from the box below and refer to the passage to fill the gaps:

Dr. Gatsby, an (1)............... psychologist, has suggested that there are problems affecting the (2)............... and society when the workplace is biased towards hiring personnel only on the basis of their qualifications on (3)............... . He claims that an over-emphasis placed on academic success is causing (4)............... in students at school and in working adults studying (5)............... . Also, more practical skills might be (6)............... by employers hiring applicants for jobs. However, the most (7)............... consequence of this preference for ever more highly qualified (8)..............., apart from a possible drop in university (9)..............., is that those who are unable to afford a (10)............... level of education are disadvantaged. Gatsby's views have not met with universal acceptance.

undesirable	individual	stress	standards	problem	worse
educational	work	paper	higher	full-time	numbers
overlooked	applicants	subject	part-time	relevant	personal

5.8 CHART COMPLETION: Refer to the reading passage in Exercise 5.3 to complete the chart below:

WHO	BELIEF	REASON
wealthy parents	It is necessary to (1)	(2) ....
politicians	We should (3)	n/a
employers	It is better to hire (4)	n/a
Dr. Gatsby	Working adults are stressed when (5)	(6) ....
most educationists	Dr. Gatsby's comments about standards are (7)	(8) ....

5.9 SHORT-ANSWER QUESTIONS: Refer to the text in Exercise 5.3.

i.   Which **4 words** in the text tell the reader that everyone knows competition is the main reason for upgrading one's qualifications? ....

ii. Which **4 words** in the text tell the reader that studying to improve one's level of education is an old idea? ....

iii. Which **2 words** tell the reader that people are reassessing the way they think about the role of education within society? ....

5.10 TRUE / FALSE / NOT GIVEN: Refer to the text in Exercise 5.3.

a. It is impossible these days to get a good job without a qualification from a respected institution.   **T   F   NG**

b. Most people who upgrade their qualifications do so for the joy of learning.   **T   F   NG**

c. In some jobs, the position you hold must be reapplied for.   **T   F   NG**

d. Some parents spend extra on their children's education because of the prestige attached to certain schools.   **T   F   NG**

e. According to the text, students who performed badly at school used to be accepted by their classmates.   **T   F   NG**

f. Employees who do not undertake extra study may find their salary decreased by employers.   **T   F   NG**

g. Citizens appear to have responded to the call by politicians to become better qualified.   **T   F   NG**

h. Britain's education system is equal to any in the world in the opinion of most educationists.   **T   F   NG**

5.11 WORD PUZZLE: Fit the words in the shaded box into the grids above it to form a sentence based on information contained in Reading Passage 5. Each letter has a unique number. Then, fill in the letters in the large circular grid and discover the message. ([0] = a space.)

Row 1: [3][12] [20][5][7][1][13][11][1]'S [6][9][14][14][10][15][7][1] [9][15]

Row 2: [8][15][2][4][10][12][1][2][7][11] [10][3][8][6][5][7][2][9][15]

Row 3: [17][10][12][10] [15][9][7] [17][10][16][16] [12][10][6][10][2][4][10][3]

Shaded box words:

well	comments	Gatsby's	not	received
education	university	were	Dr.	on

Start

Row 1: [6][12][2][7][2][6][1][0][18]P[9][2][15][7][0][9][8][7][0][7][19]H[5][7]

Row 2: [21][5][12][0][20]G[12][10][5][7][10][12][0][7][19][5][15][0][7][19][10] ... [7]

(with side column: [0] ... [0][19])

Row 3: [11] [1][0][5][7][0][7][19][10][0][7][2][14][10] *Finish* [1][10]

Row 4: [16] [10] ... [7][0]

Row 5: [16] [6][15][10][2][12][10][18][22]X[10][0][10][15][9][0][1][1][10][12][12]

Row 6: [5] ... [10]

Row 7: [8][1][8][0][10][12][5][0][11][3][8][7][1][0][21][9][0][1][3][12][5][17]

(ANSWERS ON PAGE 123)

✍️ WRITING EXERCISES 5.1 - 5.5

5.1 PHRASE INSERTION: Practice for Writing Task 1:

Insert the correct words and phrases from the flowchart below in the blank spaces in sentences 'a' to 'm' which form a model answer to the task.

The flowchart below shows the process involved in writing a formal academic essay for a particular university course.

Describe the stages of the process in a report for a university lecturer.

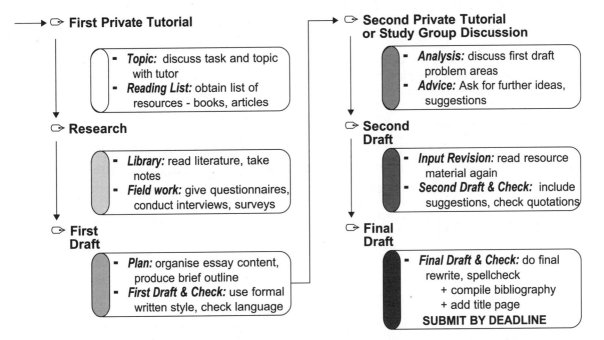

Preparation and Writing of a Formal Academic Essay

a. For this university course an essay is completed in (1)_____ .

b. (2)_____ a private tutorial in which the task and topic are fully discussed with the tutor.

c. A reading list should be obtained, detailing useful resource material.

d. The (3)_____ involves conducting suitable research.

e. Notes are taken from available literature at the library, and data collected from questionnaires, interviews and surveys.

f. (4)_____ is the third stage.

g. First, it is necessary to organise the content of the essay and produce (5)_____ .

h. Next, the draft is written in the acceptable (6)_____ and checked for appropriate language.

i. (7)_____ is another tutorial or study group discussion, during which problem areas are analysed and further ideas and suggestions are noted.

j. The fifth stage includes reading the resource material again before (8)_____ , using suggestions from stage four.

k. Once completed, all quotations should be checked for errors.

l. The sixth stage consists of writing (9)_____ of the essay.

m. (10)_____ before adding a title page and compiling a bibliography. The essay should then be submitted before the deadline for completion.

the final draft	a brief outline	writing a second draft	formal academic style
the first stage is	six stages	second stage	a spellcheck is required
stage number four	writing the first draft		

5.2 LAYOUT AND ORGANISATION: Writing Task 1:

Notice that the sentences that make up the model answer on page 87 are in the correct order but are not in paragraphs. Decide how many paragraphs the minimum 150 word description of the diagram will require.

REMEMBER: (For further advice, refer to '*101 Helpful Hints for IELTS*')

1. You do not need a separate paragraph for the introduction in the IELTS Writing Task 1. Your **general descriptive statement** can be attached to the first sentence of the body paragraph.

2. You do not need a paragraph for each stage of the process in the IELTS Writing Task 1 because the paragraphs would be too short. Combine some of the stages together in a paragraph.

3. You do not need a separate conclusion in Writing Task 1. The last stage of the process (or final description) will be sufficient. There is usually no need to conclude since you are not providing an argument or giving opinions in Writing Task 1.

Next, carefully read the '10 Point Guide to Presentation and Layout' on page 127 (reprinted from '*101 Helpful Hints for IELTS*') before writing out the model answer on the lines below by combining sentences 'a' to 'm' on page 87. Aim to present your work legibly and as neatly as possible.

WRITING TASK 1:

5.3 SENTENCE CONSTRUCTION: Writing Task 2:

A university lecturer has asked you to write an essay on the following topic:

> *'Discuss the causes and some effects of widespread drug use by young people in modern day society. Make any recommendations you feel are necessary to help fight youth drug abuse.'*

Add the nouns, noun phrases, and pronoun phrases in the brackets below to the incomplete sentences taken from the model answer to the task above. The first one has been done as an example:

a. .....*Youth drug abuse is a serious problem nowadays in many cultures.*.............

- is - nowadays in - .
(a serious problem / many cultures / youth drug abuse)

b. ....
....

Not only is - on the rise, but - are experimenting with - .
(alcohol and tobacco / children as young as 10 years old / illegal drug use)

c. ....
....

- are unclear, but - blame - .
(certain sociologists / the examples set by their elders / the reasons for this behaviour)

d. ....
....

- are, in effect, telling - that it is acceptable to abuse - with - .
(drugs / their children / their bodies / parents who drink and smoke to excess)

e. ....
....

Consequently, - may have - even if - are against - .
(children / their parents / their use / a similar view towards illegal drugs)

f. ....
....

In addition, - can only confuse - who are also taught at - that - is wrong.
(children / drug abuse / school / drug use shown on television and in films)

The sentences above constitute the introduction and the first paragraph of the body of the essay. Look at the main points of the paragraphs expressed below:

Introduction	Body Para. 1	Body Para. 2	Body Para. 3	Conclusion
youth drug use a major problem - reasons unclear	outside influences (parents, media & school) can confuse	causes: pressure at school & at home - drugs an escape	effects: on the individual & on society	recommend: solution is education, and reduce competition & pressure

5.4 PARAGRAPHS: The sentences below constitute the second and third paragraphs of the body, and the conclusion of the model essay, in the correct order but unseparated. Decide where the paragraphs should begin and end:

g. The pressure on young people to perform well at school in order to compete for jobs is a possible cause of the problem.

h. Many believe they cannot live up to their parents' expectations and feel a sense of hopelessness.

i. Also, the widespread availability of drugs means teenagers are faced with the temptation to experiment.

j. Drugs are used as a means of expressing dissatisfaction with the pressures they face in society.

k. The effects of drug abuse are well known.

l. Many young people's talents are wasted and addiction to hard drugs can cost a user his or her life.

m. Furthermore, those who drink and drive may be involved in fatal road accidents.

n. The cost to society is great, and enormous amounts of money are spent on convicting drug dealers and on education programmes.

o. To conclude, I recommend that the only sensible way to solve this problem is to educate young people about the dangers of drug use and to take steps to reduce the pressure of competition placed upon them.

5.5 LAYOUT: Writing Task 2.

Now, carefully read the '10 Point Guide to Presentation and Layout' on page 127 (reprinted from *101 Helpful Hints for IELTS*) before writing out the model essay on the lines below by combining sentences 'a' to 'o' above and on the previous page. Pay particular attention to the way in which you separate your paragraphs. (Are you using the modern or traditional method?)

WRITING TASK 2:

....

....

....

....

....

....

....

....

....

....

....

....

....

WRITING TASK 2 - continued:

....

....

....

....

....

....

....

....

....

....

....

....

....

....

....

....

....

....

....

....

....

....

....

....

....

....

....

....

(ANSWERS ON PAGES 123 - 124)

?! PUNCTUATION EXERCISES 5.1 - 5.2

5.1 PUNCTUATION (1): Place the correct punctuation marks at the points illustrated within the following texts taken from Reading Passage 5:

A ▼ striving to become better educated is hardly a new concept ▼ ▼ wealthy parents have always been willing to spend the vast amounts of extra money necessary to send their children to schools with a perceived educational edge ▼ ▼ working adults have long attended night schools and refresher courses ▼ ▼ competition for employment has been around since the curse of working for a living began ▼ ▼ is the present situation so very different to that of the past ▼

B ▼ at first glance ▼ the situation would seem to be laudable ▼ a positive response to the exhortations of politicians for us all to raise our intellectual standards and help improve the level of intelligence within the community ▼ ▼ yet there are serious ramifications according to at least one educational psychologist ▼ ▼▼ dr brendan gatsby has caused some controversy ▼ in academic circles by suggesting that a bias towards what he terms ▼ paper excellence ▼ might cause more problems than it is supposed to solve ▼ ▼ gatsby raises a number of issues that affect the individual as well as society in general ▼

C ▼ naturally ▼ although there is agreement that learning can cause stress ▼ gatsbys comments ▼▼ ▼ regarding university standards have been roundly criticised as alarmist by most educationists who point out that ▼ by any standard of measurement ▼ ▼ ▼ britains education system overall ▼ at both secondary and tertiary levels ▼ is equal to that of any in the world ▼

5.2 PUNCTUATION (2): Now punctuate the following:

studying at an english language college in a foreign country has its ups and downs for most students it is the first time they have attempted to learn another language full-time consequently it can be quite exhausting on the other hand there is the chance to meet new people and make friends from a number of countries in a short space of time the work itself is challenging the teachers although friendly are there to make sure your language requirements are achieved you must take advantage of every opportunity to put your new knowledge to the test and speak english whenever possible self-discipline regular daily practice and a relaxed attitude to learning are the keys to success

(ANSWERS ON PAGE 124)

❋ SPELLING EXERCISES 5.1 - 5.2

5.1 SPELLING ERRORS: Locate all the spelling errors in the following short passage. There are exactly 9 of them.

Young people are usually extremely critical of decisions made by persons in authority. This attitude is not always acceptable to the more powerful members of a society. They may feel threatened by the idealism of some university students; an idealism which often prevents the latter from viewing an issue objecively. Yet without student protests, certain injustices within society might never be exposed.

Although the community and the media usually atack student unrest at the time, many years later, as community attittudes change, the reasons for that student action become clearer, and generally their ideas, if not their methods, are considered more aceptable. If we can understand that it is probably in societies best interest for the young to question existing attitudes and injustices, we might realise that we would do well to listen more closely to what they have to say.

Perhaps older people should become more tolerent off the ideas and creative expression of the younger generation. Too often the ideas they express are dismissed simply becouse they are new. On the other hand, young people ought to recognise when they are being impossibly sellfish and their demands are too impractical.

5.2 WHICH SPELLING?: Place a circle around the correctly spelt version of the word from the four columns below:

acommodation	accommodation	acomodation	accomodation
appreciation	apreciation	appreceation	apreication
bussines	buziness	business	businness
developping	devellopping	develloping	developing
entertanement	entertanment	entertainment	entertainement
feasible	feasable	feesible	feesable
governmentle	governmental	govenmental	governementle
hypothetical	hypetheticle	hipothetical	hypathetical
indefenite	indefinate	indeffinite	indefinite
indiscriminite	indiscriminete	indiscriminite	indiscriminate
necessary	neccesary	nessesary	neccessary
prespective	pespective	prespective	perspective
thurough	thorough	thorrough	thourough
unsuccessful	unsucessful	unsucessfull	unsuccessfull

(ANSWERS ON PAGE 124)

GRAMMAR EXERCISES 5.1 - 5.7

5.1 COMMON ERRORS (1): Choose which **one** of the underlined parts of the following sentences is incorrect:

a. There are a number of disadvantages of learn a second language while at school.
A B C D

b. Learning a foreign language enables a student develop an understanding of another culture.
A B C D

c. The most problematical of the four major language skills are probably that of writing.
A B C D

d. Due to the increase in telecommunications, the world is, in effect, shrinking rapidly.
A B C D

e. Studying when older is much more difficult. On the contrary, it can still be rewarding.
A B C D

f. Some countries must change the way in which they taught languages in their schools.
A B C D

g. The biggest factor in producing able students must going to be the quality of the teaching.
A B C D

h. These days, the focus in schools on creative thinking is largely responsible for Australian
A B
school students lack grammatical ability.
C D

5.2 COMMON ERRORS (2): Underline all the errors in the following sentences and correct them:

a. Almost the students think that learning language is hard because of the new vocabularies.

....

b. There are another reasons why study a language is difficult for the oversea students.

....

c. I am very exciting with the chance to study the computer science in the foreign country.

....

d. It is important to practice your study with different nationality classmate if it is possible.

....

e. The chart is giving many informations of the number of student now study in Britain.

....

f. The educational system in my country is not the same with the other place.

....

g. After study, I hope to go travel over the world and enjoy to meet new peoples.

....

5.3 COMPARISON & CONTRAST (1):
Complete the chart by deciding which two things are being compared or contrasted in the following sentences. Then, note the **markers** used and state whether they are markers of comparison or contrast. First, look at the example that is done for you:

Ex: The difference between the attitude of female students and that of male students to the study of mathematics, is noticeable at an early age.

i.   A few years ago, computers were used only in business, in medicine, and for scientific research, whereas these days they are common in almost all schools.

ii.   Young people are often extremely inquisitive and creative. By comparison, the older one gets, the less inclined one is to experiment with new ideas.

iii. Male and female students are quite different to each other with regard to the age at which they begin to develop an intellectual self-discipline.

iv.   Sport is an important subject at a comprehensive school. Likewise, sporting activities should not be overlooked when a student is engaged in study at university.

v.   Youth today are nowhere near as selfish and unaware of what is happening in the world as the media would have us believe.

vi.   While it is common knowledge that European students are usually quite radical on campus, it is generally true that they work hard to complete their studies.

	ITEM 1	COMPARISON/CONTRAST MARKERS	ITEM 2
Ex:	*the attitude of female students (to the study of mathematics)*	*The difference between ... and ...* (contrast)	*that * of male students (* the attitude to the study of mathematics)*
i.			
ii.			
iii.			
iv.			
v.			
vi.			

5.4 COMPARISON & CONTRAST (2):
Now compare or contrast the items listed below using similar constructions to those used in Exercise 5.3:

❑   the education system in your country ..... & ..... the education system in Britain

❑   the teaching style in your country ..... & ..... the teaching style in Britain

❑   the competition for university places in your country ..... & ..... and in Britain

❑   the cost of tertiary education in your country ..... & ..... and in Britain

❑   a typical classroom in your country ..... & ..... and in Britain

❑   the languages taught in your high school ..... & ..... and in British comprehensive schools

You might wish to refer to the Stage 2 topics on pages 77 & 78 of *'101 Helpful Hints for IELTS'* to give you ideas for items of your own choice to compare or contrast.

5.5 SUPERLATIVES: Construct sentences expressing the absolute quality of the following people and things, according to the information in brackets:

Ex: The Eiffel Tower (size/iron tower/Europe) - The Eiffel Tower is the <u>largest iron tower</u> in Europe.

1. Ayers Rock, Australia, (big/rock/world) ....
2. Amazon River (length/river/world) ....
3. Mont. Blanc (height/mountain/Europe) ....
4. United States (affluence/nation) ....
5. China (population/country) ....
6. Diesel engine (economy/vehicle engine) ....
7. Pluto (understanding/planet in the solar system) ....
8. A score of 9 in IELTS (?) ....
9. Adolf Hitler (?) ....
10. Albert Einstein (?) ....

5.6 ADVERBS (1): Note the following types of adverbs:

a. Adverbs of degree	... make adjectives, adverbs or verbs *stronger* or *weaker*
b. Adverbs of manner	... indicate *how* something happens
c. Adverbs of place and time	... indicate *where* or *when* something happens
d. Adverbs of frequency	... indicate *how often* something happens
e. Sentence adverbs	... indicate *an attitude to the whole sentence*
f. Adverbs in phrasal verbs	... *describe the verb* (with a noun phrase following)
g. Prepositional adverbs	... *describe the verb* (with no noun phrase following)

Indicate the **type** of adverbs/adverbial phrases underlined in the text below:

The argument about (1) <u>precisely</u> who should bear the cost of educating our children has (2) <u>recently</u> surfaced in the media as a result of government efforts to (3) <u>substantially</u> cut (4) <u>back</u> the funding of comprehensive schools. But before this can be done it will become necessary to determine if the voting public will (5) <u>readily</u> accept the view that free education is no longer a basic right, and that the 'user pays' principle should apply. The government's argument is that this principle is (6) <u>frequently</u> applied elsewhere, so why not in education?

Most hope the government's plan falls (7) <u>through</u>, and few accept that parents of children at comprehensive schools should be forced to pay extra. After all, (8) <u>at present</u>, they must supply uniforms, pay for textbooks, and incur many other hidden fees. Also, the entire community (9) <u>eventually</u> benefits from money spent on education. (10) <u>In fact</u>, in that sense we are all 'users'. Nonetheless, the government is (11) <u>strongly</u> insisting that children at comprehensive schools are the immediate beneficiaries, and therefore their parents should expect to (12) <u>partially</u> foot the bill, as parents with children at private schools do in full.

(1) ..*a*.. (2) ...... (3) ...... (4) ...... (5) ...... (6) ...... (7) ...... (8) ...... (9) ...... (10) ...... (11) ...... (12) ......

5.7 ADVERBS (2): Adverbs and adverbial phrases can assist you to write informative, precise and therefore more effective sentences. They often inform the reader of the writer's feelings and attitudes to what is being said. Write some sentences which comment on the issues raised in the text in Exercise 5.6 above. Be sure to include some adverbs or adverbial phrases in your sentences.

(ANSWERS ON PAGES 124 - 125)

✪ VOCABULARY EXERCISES 5.1 - 5.3

5.1 WORD FORMATION: Complete the chart to provide the correct form of the words shown for the given parts of speech: (Not all forms are possible.)

NOUNS			ADJECTIVE	VERB	ADVERB
PLACE *	PERSON	GERUND/THING			
-				educate	-
		teaching			-
-				survey	-
-			instructive		
		studying/study			
-	-			-	ably
		practising/practice			-
	performer				-
-				assess	-
-			qualified		-
academy				-	

* double word nouns are possible

5.2 PREFIXES (1): Note the meanings of the 5 prefixes given in the box below. Then work out the approximate meaning of the words that follow before checking their meanings in a good dictionary:

trans = across, to the other side	**dis** = causes the action to be reversed
anti / **counter** = against, in opposition to	**mis** = in the wrong manner

transcontinental ....

anticlockwise ....

counterbalance ....

discount ....

disreputable ....

mishandle ....

misshapen ....

5.3 PREFIXES (2): Can you think of three more words beginning with each of the prefixes listed in the exercise above?

(ANSWERS ON PAGE 125)

⊛ IELTS QUIZ 5.1 - 5.5

5.1 BASIC INFORMATION QUIZ: Answer the following questions taken from the Introduction to IELTS in *'101 Helpful Hints for IELTS'*:

a. How long does the entire IELTS test take to complete?

    2 hours 45 minutes?   2 hours 50 minutes?   2 hours 55 minutes?

b. How long does it usually take to receive your IELTS test results?

    within one week?   within ten days?   within two weeks?

c. How many times do you hear the Listening Sub-test tape in the examination?

    once only?   twice?   three times?

d. How many passages does the Reading Sub-test consist of?

    three passages?   four passages?   any number of passages?

e. In which Writing Sub-test task might you be asked to give your opinions?

    Writing Task 1?   Writing Task 2?   both tasks?

f. How many parts are there to the Speaking Sub-test?

    three parts?   four parts?   five parts?

g. Which part of the Speaking Sub-test requires you to speak on a particular topic?

    Part 2?   Part 3?   no part of the test?

h. The Sub-tests are each marked from 0 to 9. In which tests are half marks possible?

    Reading and Listening   Writing and Speaking   all Sub-tests?

i. How long must you wait before taking the IELTS test again?

    one month?   three months?   no restriction?

5.2 LISTENING HELP QUIZ: Answer the following questions taken from the Listening Help Section in *'101 Helpful Hints for IELTS'*:

1. The secret to increasing your Listening Test skills is to:

    a. predict what you may hear

    b. listen more intensely to the tape when it is played a second time

    c. guess the answers if you are unsure

2. Clues to the answer and sometimes the answers themselves are:

    a. not heard on the tape

    b. found in print in the test booklet

    c. written on the Answer Sheet

3. When listening for an answer you should be aware that the speaker on the tape:

    a. might not speak the answer clearly

    b. could give the wrong answer

    c. may change his or her mind or correct what is said

5.3 READING HELP QUIZ: Answer the following True or False questions based on information given in the Reading Help Section of the book:

a. You must always answer the questions in the order they are presented. **T F**

b. You must write the answers on the Answer Sheet as you do the test. **T F**

c. It is wise to read the reading passages first before looking at the questions. **T F**

d. The topic sentence of a paragraph is always the first sentence. **T F**

e. The answer you are looking for is not always within the reading text itself. **T F**

f. In a gapfill task the answer you need may be repeated in the text. **T F**

g. You should continue to answer the questions in a task even though an advised time to complete the task has passed. **T F**

5.4 WRITING HELP QUIZ: Answer the following short-answer questions based on information given in the Writing Help Section of the book:

a. What should you do before you begin to write the answers to both writing tasks?

....

b. Should you always write a separate introduction and conclusion in Writing Task 1?

....

c. You should separate the question in Tasks 1 & 2 into two parts. What are they?

....

d. What is the name given to the type of paragraph included to balance an essay that requires an argument?

....

5.5 SPEAKING HELP QUIZ: From the list below, decide what one **should do** and **should not do** in the Speaking Sub-test based on information given in the Speaking Help Section of the book:

a. If the examiner shakes your hand, return his or her handshake confidently.

b. Answer questions briefly and wait for the next question.

c. Memorise a short speech on a particular topic to use in the test.

d. Organise your reply to a topic that is given to you to speak about.

e. Ask the examiner to repeat a question that you do not fully understand.

f. Read aloud the words printed on the topic prompt card given to you.

g. Try to impress the examiner with your large vocabulary and complex ideas.

h. If you have no plans for the future, explain that to the examiner.

i. After the test is over, ask the examiner to give you an idea of your speaking ability.

(ANSWERS ON PAGES 125)

TAPESCRIPTS 1.1 - 1.8 *(pages 5 - 7)*

(SIDE 1)

1.1 *Narrator:* 202 Useful Exercises for IELTS. Part One. Listening Exercise 1.1. Listen to the following sentences, pausing your machine after each sentence to write down the essential details of what you have heard:

a. Edinburgh is the capital city of Scotland.
b. The city is often regarded as the most cultured and cosmopolitan city north of London.
c. The annual Edinburgh International Festival attracts over a million visitors from all around the world.
d. The centre of the city is in two parts: the New Town and the Old Town.
e. The New Town was designed to improve upon the cramped and crowded city conditions.
f. The Old Town, medieval in style, is a maze of narrow alleyways down which sewage once ran freely.
g. The Festival is actually a concurrent series of separate arts festivals lasting for three weeks.
h. Now the largest Arts festival on Earth, it was once dominated by opera.
i. Today, festival performances range in taste from the exotic and controversial to the highly sophisticated.
j. This most romantic of cities boasts a spectacular castle, set high on top of an extinct volcanic rock.

1.2 *Narrator:* Exercise 1.2. A. Write down the numbers you hear in the following sentences:

A
i. The earliest known inhabitants established settlements in Scotland in 6000 B.C.
ii. Scotland is 275 miles long and, at its broadest point, only 150 miles wide.
iii. Edinburgh averages 140 days of rain a year, with an average of 1.89 and 2.72 inches in January and July respectively.
iv. Its average temperature in summer is 65 degrees Fahrenheit or 18 degrees centigrade.
v. Its average temperature in winter is 43 degrees Fahrenheit or 6 degrees centigrade.
vi. The original Celtic language, Gaelic, is understood by less than 2% of the Scottish population.
vii. In 1992, polls showed that 1 out of 2 Scots favoured independence from England.
viii. Edinburgh Zoo, with Scotland's largest animal collection, is set amidst 197.6 hectares of parkland.
ix. Robbie Burns, Scotland's most revered poet, was born on January 25, 1759 in a cottage in Alloway.
x. There are more than 440 golf courses in Scotland; the game being played as long ago as the 1400s.

B *Narrator:* B. Spell correctly the names of the Scottish cities and towns you hear:

i.	INVERARAY	iv.	KIRKCALDY	vii.	ABERDEEN	x. BANNOCKBURN
ii.	HELENSBURGH	v.	DUNFERMLINE	viii.	GLASGOW
iii.	FALKLAND	vi.	SKYE	ix.	LOCHINVER

C *Narrator:* C. Spell correctly the names of the following persons associated with Scotland:

i. John Knox — *(religious leader who helped shape the democratic Scottish government)*
ii. Robert Louis Stevenson — *(one of the best-loved authors of classics 'Treasure Island' and 'Kidnapped')*
iii. James Maxwell — *(scientist who discovered the laws of electrodynamics)*
iv. Andrew Carnegie — *(philanthropist who gave his name to New York's Carnegie Hall)*
v. David Livingstone — *(missionary and explorer who worked to end the slave trade in Africa)*
vi. Flora MacDonald — *(assisted Bonnie Prince Charlie to regain the British crown for Catholicism)*
vii. Mary Stuart — *(Catholic Queen of Scots; executed by Elizabeth I of England)*
viii. Dorothy Maclean — *(New Age environmentalist and spiritual founder of the Findhorn cult)*
ix. Robert Bruce — *(inspired by a tenacious spider, he drove the English from Scotland)*
x. Sir James Barrie — *(author best known for having written the classic children's story 'Peter Pan')*

D *Narrator:* D. Write down the telephone numbers of the tourist offices in the following Scottish towns:

i. Jedburgh (01835/863435)
ii. Stirling (01786/475019)
iii. Callander (01877/330342)
iv. Aberdour (01383/860325)
v. Loch Tay (01567/820397)
vi. Dunoon (01369/703785)
vii. Armadale (01471/844260)
viii. Stornaway (01851/703088)
ix. Stonehaven (01569/762806)
x. Braemar (013397/41600)

1.3 *Narrator:* Exercise 1.3. Radio Item 1:

RADIO ITEM 1

This week's controversial topic is ... 'violent video games'. Are they responsible for a rise in the number of attacks by children in the schoolyard?' Some social commentators say yes. Worse, it has been suggested that two recent killings by teenagers were prompted by the playing of video games with extreme content. But is it proven?

The jury is out on this issue. Not nearly enough research has been done to either prove or disprove that violent gaming leads to violence in children in real life. What is known is that a child who is already disturbed might certainly react violently after playing a violent computer game; but a psychotic child might just as easily react inappropriately to having seen a family video or after reading the newspaper.

Unfortunately, it is too early to say yet whether the immense amount of violence on TV and in video games has a deleterious effect on children, but one thing is certain - violence sells. And, interestingly, violence appeals far more to young male video gamers than to young female players; the latter preferring games which rely more on discovery and the development of the relationships between the characters onscreen. Does this prove that boys are somehow instinctively more violent than girls? Not necessarily. It could merely be that the way in which non-violent 'so-called girl's' games are packaged, with their pink and fluffy characters and backgrounds, does not appeal to boys. Software companies may be guilty of stereotyping when it comes to how they package their products for the two sexes.

Are violent video games merely a form of degrading entertainment? Or do they have some socially redeeming value after all? It has been argued that because computer games are interactive - gaming is not a passive activity like watching TV - they might, in fact, allow a child to indulge his or her violent fantasies and relieve pent-up frustrations in a socially acceptable and less harmful way. On the other hand, violent games may be heightening the release of tension children experience upon destroying an onscreen character; violence, instead of being punished as in the real world, is rewarded with higher scores and faster music.

So, what do you think? Let us know if you believe that violent video games lead to child violence by ringing this number now: 01256-381574. That number again … 01256-381574.

RADIO ITEM 2

Narrator: Radio Item 2:

Newsman: The latest publishing craze which has taken off all over the world, is the publication of what have come to be known as 'zines, short, of course, for 'magazines'. However, unlike magazines, whose fortunes ebb and flow, these thinner and less glossy 'zines can be desk-top published at a greatly reduced cost. Of course, 'zines are also available to be read on-line, that is, on the Internet. 'Zines are rather like comics, except that they also contain intelligent and often controversial articles on topics that interest today's highly educated youth. I spoke earlier today to Jean Cramp, the publisher of yet another desk-top magazine clone called 'Fill Me In'. Jean, can you tell us why you called your 'zine 'Fill Me In'?

Jean: Well, it's a joke really. You know, most newspapers and magazines don't tell the whole story, or at any rate, they don't talk about issues that me and my friends want to know about. So that's why we started this 'zine, you see - to 'fill the reader in' on the real news.

Newsman: So how well is your 'zine selling?

Jean: Oh, great - in fact it's only the fourth week of publication of the first issue and we've had to reprint another 2000. We've sold about 2300. Mostly in alternative bookshops that cater for people who are er … different.

Newsman: How, in fact, do you publish them?

Jean: On a computer - all the graphic work and, of course, the word-processing, too. It's pretty simple and there's only three of us in the publishing team. We work from our office which is actually in the front room at home - we were all students together at Design College you see. We've quit now to spend more time on it.

Newsman: Why do think your 'zine is such a success?

Jean: We tell it like it is, you know, we don't leave out any facts and we don't tell lies like the other media. You know, current affairs shows like this one for instance …

Newsman: Well, thank you, er … , and, well, I wish you all the best of luck with your … er … 'zine, Jean.

1.8

LECTURE 1

Narrator: Exercise 1.8. Lecture 1:

Can a new language be learnt in six weeks as some courses promise? Learning a language is not an easy task, though the reason why it is so difficult cannot be explained without an understanding of how human language is acquired, and unfortunately, no-one knows exactly how it is done. Linguists have many theories, but it is still a mystery and one that may never be fully solved. Since hard and fast facts about first language acquisition are in short supply, it is not surprising to find that there are numerous competing theories on how best to learn a second or third language. One thing is certain, though, it doesn't happen overnight. Or does it?

One theory that has been promoted for some years now is that of subliminal language learning - taking words into your mind while not consciously aware of them. Play a cassette tape of words and phrases you wish to learn while you are asleep or perhaps while driving a car. It doesn't matter if you listen to them or not, or even if the words are within your normal range of hearing. Your brain will 'hear' the words and store them deep within your mind, ready for easier extraction when you practice certain exercises containing those words and phrases.

The argument goes like this: when you learnt your own language you had been spoken to and were constantly exposed to words in that language from the day you were born and possibly even before you were born. Yes, babies react to words spoken to them inside the mother's womb. This constant exposure ensured that the words were already planted in your mind before you actually learnt them. The subliminal method, then, is based on similar principles. Even having the TV or radio on all day in another language serves the same purpose. But best results come from playing tapes with specially selected words and phrases over and over again.

Recent surveys seem to indicate that early success in learning a foreign language requires at least two other conditions to be met. First of all, the range of vocabulary you need to learn should be restricted. It has been known for decades now that most of what one needs to say everyday in the English language can be effectively communicated with a vocabulary of just 760 words. Secondly, the practice you do needs to focus on manipulations of those very same words. When starting to learn a language, reading the newspaper in that language is largely a waste of time - there are far too many new words to learn. Later, of course, reading all kinds of material in the new language is essential.

Remember that learning a language is something you have already managed. All of us are constantly, if not always consciously, engaged in increasing the knowledge of our own language, and the language itself is changing slowly every day. Language learning is a part of everyone's daily life. The only real problem with most quick-fix language learning solutions is that they do not take into account one vital difference between the learning of one's first language and the learning of other languages. And that is, people who speak different languages actually think in very different ways. No wonder students are suspicious of six week courses that promise the earth!

TAPESCRIPTS 2.1 - 2.8 *(pages 22 - 24)*

2.1 *Narrator:*   Part Two. Listening Exercise 2.1. Listen to the following sentences, pausing your machine after each sentence to write down the essential details of what you have heard:

   a.   Cardiff has been the official capital of Wales since only 1955.

   b.   This city of 270,000 people is prosperous, with a large university and an extraordinary castle.

   c.   Wales has some extremely beautiful scenery, but also some of the most depressing coal-mining towns.

   d.   More than 50% of the pits closed during the 1930s, and the last large coal mine in Wales closed in 1994.

   e.   Nuclear power stations now supply much of the energy that was once derived solely from coal.

   f.   The major industry in Wales these days is tourism, which accounts for over 10% of jobs in the region.

   g.   Cardiff was once the world's busiest coal port, producing one third of the world's coal.

   h.   The city was heavily bombed during the Second World War, because of its strategic importance.

   i.   Fortunately, since the '60s, much of the industrial damage to the Welsh environment has been reversed.

   j.   The Cardiff Bay Project, a 30 minute walk from the city centre, has rejuvenated the old dock area, and nearby mud flats have been turned into a freshwater lake.

2.2 *Narrator:*   Exercise 2.2. A.   Write down the numbers you hear in the following sentences:

A   i.   Wales is approximately 170 miles long and 60 miles wide; 8000 square miles in total.

   ii.   Over 2.9 million people live in Wales; they comprise almost 5% of the total population of Britain.

   iii.   1.8 million people (60% of the Welsh population) live in the highly industrialised South-east region.

   iv.   The Welsh language is now spoken by over 500,000 people, mostly in the north.

   v.   The distance from London to Cardiff is 155 miles and takes about 3 hours by car.

   vi.   In 1302, the conquering English king Edward I gave the the title of the Prince of Wales to his eldest son.

   vii.   Swansea, birthplace of the famous playwright and poet Dylan Thomas, is the second largest city in Wales with around 200,000 people.

   viii.   The highest peak in South Wales is Pen-y-Fan (2907 ft), but Snowdon is the highest in Wales at 3650 ft.

   ix.   The Snowdon Mountain Railway, built in 1896, will take you to the top daily in just under 60 minutes.

   x.   The Welsh village with the longest name in Britain has 58 letters in its name.

B *Narrator:*   B.   Spell correctly the longest named village in Britain. The name is one word of 58 letters long, but will be dictated in 10 parts:

LLANFAIR PWYLL GWYNGLL GOGERY CHWYRN DROBWLL LLAN TYSILIO GOGO GOCH
     i.   ii.   iii.   iv.   v.   vi.   vii.   viii.   ix.   x.

Welsh Translation: *'St Mary's Church by the pool of the white hazel trees, near the rapid whirlpool, by the red cave of the Church of St Tsilio'.*

C *Narrator:*   C.   Spell correctly the names of the following persons associated with Wales:

   i.   Athelstan   - *(Anglo-Saxon king of England, reluctantly accepted by the Welsh kings as their leader, so that they could be saved from the Viking invaders)*

   ii.   Owain Glyndwr   - *(leader of last revolt against England; defeated by Henry IV)*

   iii.   Richard Trevithick   - *(his engine made the world's first train journey in Wales in 1804)*

   iv.   William Burges   - *(architect and interior designer of Cardiff Castle in the late 19th century)*

   v.   Saunders Lewis   - *(one of Wales' greatest modern writers; founded the Welsh National Party)*

   vi.   Gwynfor Evans   - *(charismatic political leader of the Welsh National Party)*

   vii.   Augustus John   - *(Wales' most famous artist - particularly of portraits)*

   viii.   Dylan Thomas   - *(probably the best-known and loved of Welsh writers; died in America while on a literary tour - of an overdose of whisky)*

   ix.   Shirley Bassey   - *(internationally acclaimed singer, born in the docklands of Cardiff)*

   x.   Richard Burton   - *(famed Hollywood actor; twice married to Elizabeth Taylor)*

D *Narrator:*   D.   Write down the telephone numbers of the following Welsh Youth Hostels:

   i.   Cardiff (01222-462303)   v.   Harlech (01341-241287)   ix.   Monmouth (01600-715116)

   ii.   Swansea (01792-390706)   vi.   Pen-y-Pass (01286-870428)   x.   Aberystwyth (0197085-693)

   iii.   Brecon (01874-665270)   vii.   Saundersfoot (01834-812333)

   iv.   Bala (01678-521109)   viii.   St David's (01437-720345)

2.3 *Narrator:*   Exercise 2.3. Radio Item 3:

RADIO ITEM 3   *Announcer:* Today's edition of 'PlanetWatch' brings you our latest world environmental report. This week, Troy Hartwell takes a brief look at the most precious substance on Earth: water.

Troy: The surface of our planet is two-thirds water, of which 97% is seawater and therefore undrinkable; a further 2% is ice - unusable - that is, because it is locked up in the polar icecaps. This leaves a comparatively minute area of 12,600 cubic kilometres of fresh water, scattered unevenly about the globe, for drinking, bathing and other personal use. Of course, by far the largest percentage of available fresh water is used for farming - over 70% -

while industry consumes up to 25%.

The major problem is that our water is far too easily contaminated in a world which produces a staggering amount of pesticides from agriculture as well as industrial waste from manufacturing plants - a large proportion of which ends up in the rivers and streams that feed the reservoirs we rely on to supply us with fresh water. In addition, in many poor and developing countries of the world, sewage is added untreated to flowing and non-flowing water sources causing devastating outbreaks of disease and, sadly, more than 25,000 deaths per day. One startling statistic, which shows the extent of water pollution in a major nation, is taken from a recent United Nations report which estimates that over 78% of people in China drink from polluted water supplies.

Unfortunately, the enormous efforts that humankind has taken to provide plentiful fresh water for all - I refer to the more than 35,000 large dam and hydro-electric turbine construction projects throughout the world - these might well be ultimately responsible for falling water tables, the shrinking of natural lakes, and shrivelling rivers everywhere. One consequence of artificially diverting massive amounts of water is the loss of trees, plants and wildlife that depend on wet areas that are fast drying up. It is clear the 21st century's greatest challenge will be to reverse these worrying trends towards a drier and, therefore, dirtier world. Troy Hartwell for 'Planet Watch'.

Announcer: School project kits on this week's topic are available by telephoning this number now: 0171-825-992. I'll repeat that number ... 0171-825-992.

RADIO ITEM 4

Narrator: Radio Item 4:

This is 'Postcards from the Edge of the World'. I'm Catherine Small with a disturbing story from the Great Barrier Reef in Northern Queensland, Australia. Residents of the sleepy beachside town of Carrsville near the luxurious resort of Port Charles were woken yesterday at 6.20 a.m. to the sound of a number of explosions that many were convinced was either a serious thunderstorm, blasts of gas or even planes nose-diving into the sea! It turned out, however, that the sounds heard were actually part of a series of 25 controlled explosions set off approximately 200 metres offshore and conducted by marine authorities in an attempt to rid the sea of dangerous swarms of Portuguese Man-O'-War jellyfish that have been plaguing the local beaches for the past two years.

No-one is certain why the jellyfish have made a home in the once clear blue waters near the popular resort, but what is certain is that something had to be done. The town relies almost exclusively on the resort and tourism for its survival; but Carrsville beach has been strewn with the deadly jellyfish now for the last two summers, and fishing and bathing are no longer possible. Last year, the Shire Council decided to enlist the help of Professor Stephen Blunt, a British marine biologist working with the biology department at the University of Northern Queensland, who proposed a controversial solution to the problem involving the foreshortening of the 2 kilometre long rock shelf that lies 200 metres out to sea. The shelf apparently traps the creatures before they have the chance to escape back to the ocean and this, in turn, encourages them to increase in numbers.

Global warming is thought to be at least partly responsible for slight changes in the recent patterns of moon tides which have, however, been enough to upset the delicate natural balance - allowing the jellyfish to reach the shore in numbers previously unheard of. By blasting away almost half of the rock shelf, Professor Blunt hopes the jellyfish will soon be a thing of the past. If the technique is successful, it may be used along other sensitive coastal waters of Northern Queensland. Environmentalist groups are observing the experiment with caution.

2.8 LECTURE 2

Narrator: Exercise 2.8. Lecture 2:

To be living at the start of the new millenium is to exist in the most advanced technological era in history. It is easy to forget that we are still surrounded by countless opportunities to get close to the earth, the sea and all the other wonders of the natural environment. But for how long? Fortunately, the agricultural and industrial excesses of the past fifty years are beginning to be reversed, and, with the establishment of such watchdog organisations as Greenpeace and the World Wildlife Fund, it is likely that government policies which threaten the environment will come under ever-increasing scrutiny. Environmental agreements involving a concensus of world nations once thought impossible promise reductions in levels of so-called 'Greenhouse' gases, and the banning of the production of substances which interfere with key eco-processes such as those which deplete the ozone layer.

In Britain, perhaps the most encouraging sign is the recent change in political thinking, even among the conservative elements of the major political parties. Though once there was believed to be little political sense in pushing environmental policies in elections, 'green' political parties with policies geared towards saving the environment are supported by a significant number of electors whose views can therefore make a lasting difference.

However, there is still much to be done and little room for complacency. Unchecked consumerism in developed nations, and the destruction of virgin hardwood forests in developing countries for short-term financial gain are but two examples of issues where greed is the direct cause of environmental ruin. But what is often overlooked, even by well-intentioned 'forces for the good' such as Greenpeace, is that the best recipe for failure is poverty.

Economic growth and technological progress are not the enemies of environmental protection, but the means by which protection programmes can be implemented and conservation attained. High-tech solutions ranging from cheaper food production to safer waste disposal, from cleaner cars to more efficient energy sources - these can only come about if economic growth continues. It is very much in our interest to help make the world a richer, and therefore more environmentally-friendly, place to live.

TAPESCRIPTS 3.1 - 3.9 (pages 41 - 43)

3.1 *Narrator:*   Part Three. Listening Exercise 3.1. Listen to the following sentences, pausing your machine after each sentence to write down the essential details of what you have heard:

   a.   Manchester, one of the most important cities in England, is considered by some the northern capital.

   b.   Situated in the northwest, 39 miles inland, Manchester is the third largest urbanised area in England.

   c.   Technological innovation during the Industrial Revolution enabled the city to become the world's major cotton-milling centre in the 19th century.

   d.   Unfortunately, this rapid industrialisation brought prosperity only to the owners of the many factories.

   e.   The rise of Communism overseas was, in part, a reaction against the exploitation of workers in Manchester.

   f.   Eventually, the city declined in importance, but cotton goods are still known worldwide as manchester goods.

   g.   Liverpool, now the sixth largest city in England, was the second major city of the British Empire.

   h.   The Liverpool docks were once the site of the busiest shipbuilding activity in the world.

   i.   Both cities boast impressive museums documenting the good and bad uses of industrial technology.

   j.   Manchester and Liverpool are these days thriving centres of activity and club entertainment for youth.

3.2 *Narrator:*   Exercise 3.2. A.   Write down the numbers you hear in the following sentences:

A   i.   Manchester is 185 miles distance from London and 35 miles from Liverpool.

   ii.   Over 10 million passengers passed through Manchester Airport in 1997.

   iii.   The new 2400-seater Bridgewater Hall houses northern England's best orchestra, the Hallé.

   iv.   The first steam-operated cotton mill opened in Manchester in 1783.

   v.   The University of Manchester has over 18,000 students and almost 3000 academic staff.

   vi.   Manchester's Museum of Science and Industry is open 7 hours a day from 10 a.m. to 5 p.m.

   vii.   Inside is a working replica of a very early steam train, *The Planet*, built in 1830 and with a speed of 30 mph.

   viii.   Liverpool stretches about 13 miles along the River Mersey, but the city centre is only $1\frac{1}{4}$ square miles in size.

   ix.   The population of Liverpool peaked in 1931 at 855,000; today it is just over 519,000.

   x.   For over 400 years, tens of millions of African slaves were shipped through Liverpool bound for America.

B   *Narrator:*   B.   Spell correctly the names of these towns and cities in the Northwest of England:

i.	BLACKPOOL	iv.	LANCASTER	vii.	BOLTON	x.	PRESTON
ii.	WARRINGTON	v.	KNUTSFORD	viii.	NORTHWICH		
iii.	CREWE	vi.	HEYSHAM	ix.	CLITHEROE		

C   *Narrator:*   C.   Spell correctly the names of the following persons associated with Manchester and Liverpool:

   i.   King John   -   *(gave Liverpool a Royal Charter in 1207; chief port for trade with Ireland)*

   ii.   John Kay   -   *(inventor of the flying shuttle in 1733 which began the revolution in spinning)*

   iii.   Richard Arkwright   -   *(patented a machine for spinning cotton thread in 1769)*

   iv.   George Stephenson   -   *(his locomotive was the first to be used on the Liverpool-Manchester Railway)*

   v.   William Lever   -   *(English soap maker and industrialist who built a Sunlight soap factory)*

   vi.   Friedrich Engels   -   *(manager of textile factory in Manchester, and co-founder of Communism)*

   vii.   Alfred Waterhouse   -   *(designed the imposing Victorian neo-Gothic Town Hall in Manchester)*

   viii.   Ford Madox Brown   -   *(painter, whose series of frescoes depict historical events in Manchester)*

   ix.   Keir Hardie   -   *(politician who urged workers to strike leading to riots in Liverpool in 1911)*

   x.   John Lennon   -   *(Liverpudlian singer, whose songwriting career helped create worldwide acceptance of working-class ethics; murdered in New York in 1980)*

D   *Narrator:*   D.   Use abbreviations to quickly note down the distances and rail travel times of the following cities in the north of England:

   i.   Shrewsbury (1 hour from Manchester)   vi.   Lincoln ($1\frac{3}{4}$ hours from London)

   ii.   Chester (17 miles south of Liverpool)   vii.   York (188 miles north of London)

   iii.   Liverpool ($2\frac{1}{2}$ hours from London)   viii.   Liverpool (25 minutes from Manchester)

   iv.   Leeds (75 miles north-east of Liverpool)   ix.   York (2 hours from London)

   v.   Shrewsbury (68 miles east of Manchester)   x.   Lincoln (132 miles north of London)

3.3 *Narrator:*   Exercise 3.3. Radio Item 5:

RADIO ITEM 5   Welcome to 'Software World' - bringing you the very latest information on what is currently available on CD-ROM. Are you a director or producer looking for an unusual actor to play a part in a new movie project, or with that special look for a new commercial on TV? OK. The usual procedure would be to contact a theatrical agency who would try and sell you the idea of using one of the actors listed on their books. Books? Too old-fashioned for you? Then get yourself a copy of this latest electronic database called 'The Electronic Curtain'.

The brainchild of casting agent Fred Harkney of the Better Talent Agency, he says he got the idea of an actor's directory from his son playing computer games. Noting that junior had to type in the details of the characters in his favourite game, he realised he could do the same for the actors he represents. Eventually, he came to include information on nearly three quarters of the approximately 34,000 actors registered and looking for work in Britain. With some agencies boasting that they represent over 500 performers, the need for this product is not hard to fathom. It can be a nightmare trying to remember just which actor has done what, or just what an actor can do.

The database lists details of over 5500 actors: TV shows they have appeared in, special skills they possess - everything down to the colour of their eyes and other distinguishing physical features. By entering the details of the type of person you are looking for, the database quickly locates only those persons with the particular qualities requested.

One problem though, is that many actors feel it is too impersonal, and they could be missing out on much needed auditions for parts in theatrical shows. On the other hand, it might just get them that elusive job. The days of nervous nail-biting while waiting around to give an audition could well and truly be over. And all because of a small plastic disk. For product details ring this number now: 0171-379-6000. That number again ... 0171-379-6000.

RADIO ITEM 6

Narrator: Radio Item 6:

Welcome to 'Inventors' Corner'. This week we take a look at an invention that may well change the way in which you listen to your television set. Four years and twenty thousand pounds later, Susan Schofield of Cardiff, Wales, believes she has the answer to that nagging problem of listening to advertisements at twice the volume of the program you are watching. Annoyed at having to reach for the remote control every time an advertisement comes on the screen simply to avoid being deafened, she came up with the idea of a small device that detects when an advert is being shown, and automatically reduces the volume to a preset level. Why not cut out the sound completely? Well, that's possible if you wish, but too often, of course, the viewer misses the first few seconds of the show returning to the screen. Now, the volume is totally at your control.

Just how the device works is a patented secret, but together with her husband, a television repairman by trade, she was able to create an electronic box no bigger than your thumb that attaches to the back of the remote control itself. The only drawback is the remote must always be pointed directly at the TV set. However, Susan doesn't think this will detract from its selling power, and Susan ought to know. It was she who invented that other best-selling gadget we featured on the show two years ago. I refer, of course, to the telephone answering machine that automatically answers with a message that changes depending on the voice of the caller. Looks like Susan's done it again, with what she calls the 'Ad Subtractor'.

3.8 DICTATION 1

Narrator: Exercise 3.8. Dictation 1:

Air pollution / is probably the modern world's greatest threat. / Water can be filtered, / land can be cleared, / but filthy air can only be filtered / by the nose and lungs. / It is estimated / that living in a big city / is equivalent to smoking / half a packet of cigarettes a day. / What is more, / the most dangerous components of air pollution / are invisible gases. / We cannot smell or see / the dangerous gases given off / from the exhausts / of cars, lorries and buses. / However, / this does not mean / they are not present in our bloodstream / every time we take a breath. / It is obvious / that our future health / depends on the development / of a safer vehicle engine.

(SIDE 2)

3.9 LECTURE 3

Narrator: Exercise 3.9. Lecture 3:

Electric cars? Solar-powered buses? When most people imagine solutions to the problems of city air pollution they probably think of electricity and solar power. But the problem with an electric car is that the electrical energy stored within the batteries has to be first produced by conventional means such as burning coal, which creates the very problem the car is supposedly designed to avoid. Even the battery disposal is an environmental hazard. As for solar power, at present the solar panels that catch the sunlight are twice as big as the cars they power. And speeds of ten kilometres an hour are hardly practical. What is required is a safe, cheap and highly efficient engine that produces fewer major air pollutants and only in small quantities. You may be surprised that the answer has been with us for quite some time.

The probable solution to city air pollution is a concept for an engine that was first proposed by a French scientist in 1824 and later designed and patented by a German refrigeration engineer in 1892, whose name was Rudolph Diesel. His design for an engine that would produce more energy output but burn less fuel became known as the diesel engine. Most people think of diesel engines as being efficient and cheaper to run but smelly and rather noisy. It is true that the black soot emitted from the exhausts of diesel lorries does not naturally lead us to conclude that the diesel engine can eradicate air pollution, but, contrary to popular belief, they emit far fewer of all the major air pollutants than petrol-driven engines, except for nitrogen oxides and black soot. However, soot can be trapped, and already new diesel engines are under development, being redesigned to burn diesel fuel in such a way that the nitrogen oxide gases are released into the air as harmless nitrogen and oxygen.

In fact, if all cars were running on diesel fuel, air pollution in major cities would disappear overnight. Why then has it taken this long to do something about it? The problem is that the disadvantages of diesel engines, which include greater noise and vibration as well as taking longer to start up, have meant that car manufacturers have been reluctant to invest in production of more expensive diesel-powered cars - afraid that customers would not purchase their products. Fortunately, new technology is ensuring that diesel-powered engines become lean, clean and mean. It might not be long before city smog is but a distant memory.

TAPESCRIPTS 4.1 - 4.9 *(pages 60 - 62)*

4.1 *Narrator:*   Part Four. Listening Exercise 4.1. Listen to the following sentences, pausing your machine after each sentence to write down the essential details of what you have heard:

a.   London is the capital city of Great Britain.
b.   The Romans established what they called Londinium in 43 AD.
c.   The city is by far the largest in Europe covering an area of approximately 620 square miles.
d.   London is the political and financial heart of the nation.
e.   The Houses of Parliament building stands on the banks of the River Thames.
f.   Members of Parliament representing their electors debate changes to law within the House of Commons.
g.   The City of London, also called the Square Mile, has been the financial centre since the Middle Ages.
h.   The Bank of England was built in 1694 to fund the war with France.
i.   Most of the important money markets had their origin in sixteenth-century coffee shops.
j.   Much of the architecture of London was built in the nineteenth century during the reign of Queen Victoria.

4.2 *Narrator:*   Exercise 4.2. A.   Write down the numbers you hear in the following sentences:

A i.   During the reign of Elisabeth I, the population of London doubled from 100,000 to 200,000.
ii.   The population of London today is anything from 7 to 12 million, depending on how the count is taken.
iii.   The number of visitors to London each year is 20 million and growing.
iv.   Unfortunately, many medieval, Tudor, and Jacobean buildings were destroyed in 1666 by the Great Fire.
v.   During the Second World War, hundreds of fine 17th, 18th and 19th century buildings were bombed.
vi.   All but two of the monarchs since 1066 have been crowned in Westminster Abbey.
vii.   The clock tower next to the Houses of Parliament, containing the $13\frac{1}{2}$ ton bell called Big Ben, is 320 feet tall.
viii.   The Prime Minister's residence at No. 10 Downing St. is a fifteen minute walk from Westminster Bridge.
ix.   The changing of the guard at Buckingham Palace can be viewed at 11am and 4pm weekdays and Saturdays.
x.   Nelson's Column, a 185-foot pillar, on top of which is a statue of the famous Admiral, was built in 1805.

B *Narrator:*   B.   Spell correctly the names of the following places in and around London:

i.	TOTTENHAM	iv.	TWICKENHAM	vii.	WEMBLEY	x.	WANDSWORTH
ii.	PUTNEY	v.	LEWISHAM	viii.	ROTHERHITHE		
iii.	HARROW	vi.	ISLINGTON	ix.	GREENWICH		

C *Narrator:*   C.   Spell correctly the names of the following persons associated with London:

i.   Queen Boudicca   - *(attacked and destroyed the city in 61AD)*
ii.   William the Conqueror   - *(assumed the seat of power in London in the eleventh century)*
iii.   Sir Christopher Wren   - *(architect best remembered for St. Paul's Cathedral)*
iv.   William Shakespeare   - *(playwright whose plays were performed at the old Globe Theatre)*
v.   Winston Churchill   - *(Conservative Prime Minister who conducted the war from a London bunker)*
vi.   Geoffrey Chaucer   - *(early poet and first person to be buried in Westminster Abbey)*
vii.   Sir Arthur Conan Doyle   - *(creator of 'Sherlock Holmes', detective who lived in Baker Street)*
viii.   Sir Henry Tate   - *(inventor of the sugar cube and tycoon who founded the Tate Gallery)*
ix.   Wynkyn de Worde   - *(pupil of Caxton who moved the latter's printing presses to Fleet Street)*
x.   Diana, Princess of Wales   - *(self-annointed 'People's Princess' whose funeral stopped London in 1997)*

D *Narrator:*   D.   Use abbreviations to quickly note down the rail distances and directions from London of the following places:

i.   Manchester (184 miles north-west)   vi.   Liverpool (193 miles north-west)
ii.   Cardiff (155 miles east)   vii. Penzance (280 miles south-west)
iii.   Birmingham (110 miles north-west)   viii. Cambridge (54 miles north)
iv.   Salisbury (83 miles south-west)   ix.   Oxford (57 miles north-west)
v.   Lincoln (131 miles north)   x.   Bath (106 miles west)

4.3 *Narrator:*   Exercise 4.3. Radio Item 7:

RADIO ITEM 7   With me today from the Home Office, is Mr. David Thorpe, who has agreed to answer recent criticism of the government's handling of the so-called 'immigration problem'. The face of Britain changed radically during the latter part of the twentieth century. Since large-scale immigration of non-English-speaking persons to Britain began in the 1950s, there have been few attempts by the government to calm people's fears of an invasion of foreign languages. Yet recent research by linguists from a prominent university has revealed that in certain city areas English is almost totally unspoken, and has called into question the value of bringing non-English-speaking immigrants to this country in the future. Mr. Thorpe, why do we have a problem with English within ethnic commmunities, and is there a real danger that the English language will lose its dominance in Britain?

Thorpe: Let me begin by saying that this whole issue of people ... what was it I read in the papers? ... by the year 2050 the majority of people in the top 3 British cities would not be speaking English ... is a myth ... er, complete nonsense. The research was, in fact, conducted by a group of academics whose work was, first of all, totally misrepresented by the press, and, secondly, based on improbable statistical evidence supposedly linking language-learning difficulties to unemployment. The reverse is actually true, since ... without a job ... if you need to learn English, you can spend a greater amount of time studying in our English-language training programmes.

Newswoman: But the research points out that in certain poor areas of some large cities, English is already no longer the most commonly spoken language. What's the government doing to rectify this situation?

Thorpe: What the research actually said was that it was taking longer for some new foreign residents in Britain to become proficient in English than in the past ...

Newswoman: ... because, they say, of a drop in funding for English-language training programmes ...

Thorpe: Not at all. The percentage of funding for English courses has significantly increased under this government. No, the reason some foreigners are taking longer to learn English is that overall there has been a slight upward age shift in new migrants to city areas. It is, of course, more difficult to learn a language when you are older.

Newswoman: So will English ever become a second language in Britain, the country of its origin?

Thorpe: Really! How can that happen when the total number of immigrants to this country is a mere 50,000 a year? And that includes many who speak equally as well as you or I.

Newswoman: You or me ...

Thorpe: If not better! *(laughs)*

Newswoman: Mr. Thorpe, thank you for your time. Enquiries for English language courses can be made by telephoning this number now: 0171-389-4204. That number again ... 0171-389-4204.

RADIO ITEM 8

Narrator: Radio Item 8:

They said it would be a horror budget, and they were right: cigarettes, wine and spirits, petrol, and luxury cars - all up on July 1 - and a reversal of pre-budget policy in which we were promised that there would be no increase in the cost of a television licence. In fact, the 20% rise in the cost of a packet of cigarettes came as a surprise, since cigarettes rose by more than 30% in the last budget. The cost of subsidised health care is to be paid for from this increase, which has angered many smokers still reeling from the previous price hike. However, this will make it possible to fund much needed equipment in city and country hospitals - a pre-election pledge by the government. Wine importers, who were hoping for a modest rise of only 2% in import tax, have been slugged with a 7% increase to be phased in over 3 years. Spirits are up by 15%, and only beer manufacturers can heave a sigh of relief. Petrol, however, is set to rise by 2p a gallon, which will inevitably mean an increase in the distribution costs of most manufactured goods. Luxury cars, that is cars with a wholesale price of more than £25,000, will now incur an 8% luxury goods tax increase in September, with a further 2% increase to take effect December 1 - a total increase of 10%. One unexpected increase is in the price of a television licence - designed to offset the increased educational cost to the government of recent computer purchases in primary schools. A 1.25% rise was considered last year but was quickly dropped when elderly lobby groups reacted angrily to the proposed increase. The government is not expecting opposition to the present rise of 0.5% because the elderly will benefit substantially from the health care subsidy increases, and the gradual phasing out of stamp duties on funerals - a 3.5% drop over 5 years, which is, perhaps, the only good news in the budget.

4.8 DICTATION 2

Narrator: Exercise 4.8. Dictation 2:

A modern democracy / is founded upon three basic principles. / First, every citizen must have representation in government. / Second, voting rights shall be equal / and not recognise class distinctions. / Third, minority views will be heard and tolerated. / Most developed and economically successful nations / claim to owe their economic success / to the democratic foundations / of their political institutions. / Supporters argue that, / as well as being the most fair form of government, / it is also the most likely / to produce economic stability and prosperity. / Nevertheless, an elected government / must spend much of its time / arguing its position on an issue, / rather than implementing policy / and producing the desired result.

4.9 LECTURE 4

Narrator: Exercise 4.9. Lecture 4:

Interviewer: Will you please welcome Vernon Applethwaite, a lecturer in political science at Worthington University, California, who is here today to discuss the types of voting systems in existence in various democracies worldwide. The floor is yours, Vernon.

Vernon: It's a pleasure to be here. Well, first of all, as most of you know, countries such as Britain and the United States employ a 'winner-takes-all' system of voting. That means the candidate with the greatest percentage of votes wins the election. 'First past the post' we say; like a horse in a horserace. But that usually means that the majority of voters didn't actually vote for the winning candidate! Now is that fair? Some countries don't believe it is fair, and there are numbers of other types of voting systems in use throughout the democratic world today which attempt to better determine the will of the people. These other voting systems use what is called 'proportional representation', which is best explained by showing you a voting card. Here you can see that to the right of each candidate's name is a small box. In that box, a voter puts a number 1, 2, 3, 4 etc. and so ranks his or her preference for each candidate in numerical order. Proportional representation ensures that parties with a majority of votes will earn a majority of seats in government, but that voters in the minority will also earn their fair share of representation. At present, this doesn't happen in 'winner-takes-all' systems, where votes for minority parties are virtually disregarded. The critical difference here is that in a proportional representation system supporters of minority parties realise their votes are not being wasted and, therefore, are more likely to exercise their right to vote ... something they might not do - unless, of course, they are compelled to vote by law, as they are in Australia, for instance, but not in Britain.

Now, there are 2 main types of proportional representation systems: those that are based on voting for candidates, and those that are based on voting for political parties who later decide - after the election - which persons will fill their party's share of the seats won - seats in government, that is.

Most well-established democracies use proportional representation - in all countries in Europe except France and the United Kingdom - but such systems do vary enormously. Australia and Ireland are two countries which vote for candidates; the federal system in Germany, on the other hand, is a mixed system.

Of course, proportional representation is not without criticism. In countries such as Israel and Italy, proportional representation is responsible for the large number of small political parties and ensuing confusion and division. Another criticism is that ticking long lists of preferences for lesser-favoured candidates requires far greater political knowledge than most voters have or wish to have. Therefore, the accuracy of preferences can be called into question. However, in the main, proportional representation has decided advantages.

Interviewer: Thank you Vernon. That was quite illuminating. Next week, Vernon will return to discuss the problematical issue of whether voting should or should not be compulsory. Now, any questions?

TAPESCRIPTS 5.1 - 5.7 *(pages 79 - 81)*

5.1 *Narrator:* Part Five. Listening Exercise 5.1. Listen to the following talk about two famous universities in England. Complete the table with the essential details of what you hear:

The universities of Oxford and Cambridge are justifiably world famous. Situated 83 miles from each other, and 56 and 55 miles from London respectively, both universities are at the heart of the architecturally beautiful cities they dominate. Oxford University, founded in the late 11th century, is only a one a half hour train journey from London (the River Thames is close by), and has 36 colleges, 13,000 undergraduates and a number of important libraries and museums. The Ashmolean Museum is the oldest public museum in the country. Steeped in history, the city of Oxford, with a population of over 120,000, is flooded with thousands of tourists throughout the year, who come to see such famous colleges as University College and Queen's College; the former being known for such famous alumni as the poet Shelley and President Bill Clinton. Regrettably, women have only been granted degrees from Oxford since 1920. At Cambridge University, on the other hand, only 3 colleges accepted women until the mid 1970s; some holding out until the late 1980s. Then again, Cambridge has 7 colleges founded by women. Cambridge University was founded later than Oxford, in the 13th century, but can boast one of the most spectacular buildings in Europe - King's College, also famous for its Boy's Choir. Other important colleges at Cambridge include Trinity College (Isaac Newton and Prince Charles were among those who attended) and Jesus College. The city of Cambridge, situated on the River Cam, has a population of just 100,000 and is a much more quiet and peaceful place than Oxford, drawing fewer tourists. The rivalry between the two universities culminates in an annual boat race, which, because of the crowds, is nowadays held in London.

5.2 *Narrator:* Exercise 5.2. Lecture 5:

LECTURE 5 Today, I wish to give you a look at the first day or two in London as seen through the eyes of a young visitor to the country on a temporary student visa. For most visitors, the first taste of England is touchdown at Heathrow International Airport which is only a £20 taxi fare from the heart of the city. As soon as one gets off the plane, the busy, commercial atmosphere of London immediately becomes apparent. The traffic is dense, and moves slowly. The buildings are old and the weather is usually cloudy. Many students arrange to stay with an English family while they study at an English language college, and are therefore met at the airport.

Having met the family and settled into his or her new home - most families in the city live in semi-detached houses - a visitor is usually tired after the trip and takes a day or two to recover from jet lag. But it isn't long before the desire to look around and discover the sights and sounds of London overcomes the shock of being in a foreign country. First on the list is a trip to the college chosen while overseas as the place to study English in Britain. Most colleges are located close to the city and are surprisingly modern and welcoming. They are always within easy travel distance of a bus route or a tube station, and the buses are modern and comfortable, although it is more expensive than taking a train. Most commuters to the city prefer the tube because the system is extensive and a lot faster and cheaper.

On intake day, students gather in the common room of their chosen college and are given an orientation to the programme they are about to embark upon. After they have been welcomed to the college, and know a little more about how the school works, it is time to take a short test to determine the best class for them to begin their studies. Come lunchtime, of course, it is necessary to find a place to eat. Some students sensibly bring their own lunch or else find a restaurant nearby that suits their palate. Of course, London has a vast number of restaurants at which to choose food from countries all over the world, and prices are generally quite acceptable.

In the afternoon, a student usually discovers that the way in which the language is taught in a British environment is different to what they are used to in their home country. Some students might be surprised at the difference in teaching methods. Students in English colleges are always treated as adults and the onus to perform is therefore on the student. Attending their first lesson of the course, they meet their classmates for the next few weeks. It is time to get to know each other and the opportunity for an exchange of personal information. After class, students make their way home, enlightened and sometimes a little confused about what is expected of them. But most agree that the experience they have had on their first day of college is worth all the hardship of leaving the comfort of home.

5.4   *Narrator:*   Exercise 5.4. Dictation 3:

DICTATION 3   Studying at an English language college / in a foreign country / has its ups and downs. / For most students / it is the first time / they have attempted to learn / another language full-time. / Consequently, / it can be quite exhausting. / On the other hand, / there is the chance to meet new people / and make friends from a number of countries / in a short space of time. / The work itself is challenging; / the teachers, although friendly, / are there to make sure / your language requirements are achieved. / You must take advantage / of every opportunity / to put your new knowledge to the test / and speak English whenever possible. / Self-discipline, / regular daily practice, / and a relaxed attitude to learning / are the keys to success.

5.5   *Narrator:*   Exercise 5.5. Conversation 1:

CONVER-   *Ilsa:*   Hi, Erica. How did you go in the IELTS test? You took it two weeks ago, didn't you?

SATION 1   *Erica:*   Yes, Ilsa. It was certainly a new experience for me. I didn't do too well. It was quite a long day and I was very nervous.

Ilsa: Did you do any specific practice for the test?

Erica: No, nothing special. I just studied vocabulary by myself in the local library.

Ilsa: Maybe you should have taken a short course like I did. The teacher was very helpful and gave us a lot of practice tests. I felt quite confident when I took the test.

Erica: You always are. I often listen to you on the campus radio station. Your IELTS score got you into uni, didn't it? How is it going?

Ilsa: It's much more difficult than I expected. I have to do so much reading, and the assignments I have to write are over 2000 words long.

Erica: I thought the IELTS Writing Tasks were extremely hard to understand.

Ilsa: Yes, Erica. But that's why you should have done a practice course.

Erica: I didn't know anything about the essay topic. I had never thought about it before.

Ilsa: What was the topic?

Erica: Something to do with computers. But I know nothing about computers.

Ilsa: We studied possible topics like that in the practice course. You only need to make 2 or 3 main points about a topic, you know, because the IELTS essay task is only 250 words long. You don't have to be an expert.

Erica: I didn't like the Listening Test either. It was very fast and I couldn't catch what they were saying at all.

Ilsa: Do you listen to English every day?

Erica: Not really …

Ilsa: You live with friends from your own country, don't you?

Erica: Well, yes …

Ilsa: You really ought to be in contact with English-speaking people every day, if you want to improve fast.

Erica: I know. Maybe that's why I found the Speaking Test difficult as well.

Ilsa: What did they ask you?

Erica: Oh, many things. It all happened so fast I can't remember. Something about public transport and the

202 Useful Exercises for IELTS

course I want to study - international trade.

Ilsa:　Did you have to do a role-play?

Erica:　What's that?

Ilsa:　Pretending you're in a situation, and then you have to ask questions to find out some information.

Erica:　Oh, yes. That's right. I was at an airport or something. Anyway, I had this speech prepared about the weather in my country and my hobbies, and she never asked me about it. I tried to start talking about it but I didn't get the chance. The examiner didn't seem interested.

Ilsa:　It's meant to be a natural conversation, Erica. So what was your overall score?

Erica:　Oh, I can't tell you. I am too embarrassed.

Ilsa:　Are you going to sit for the test again?

Erica:　I have to wait twelve weeks. But, yeah.

Ilsa:　You'd better enrol in a practice course soon. In three months you should be able to increase your overall Band Score by about one band.

Erica:　I certainly hope so.

5.7　*Narrator:*　Exercise 5.7. Conversation 2. Linda and Ross are two university tutors. Follow the direction of the tour Linda will give her students on the map shown. As you listen, fill in the names of the buildings she will visit, and the time she must arrive at or leave each destination.

CONVER-SATION 2

Ross:　Ah, Linda. Thank goodness you're here. I don't know how to thank you for doing this. The student intake this semester was twice as many as expected. Over 100. I couldn't possibly take them all round the university campus myself. And the orientation tour is pretty important.

Linda:　No problem, Ross. I'm glad to help out. How are we going to do it?

Ross:　Well, I thought I'd split the students into two groups - A and B - and go in opposite directions. The A group can be yours - the Fashion and Textile students, and the B group can be mine, the nurses.

Linda:　Sounds like a good idea.

Ross:　You go in a clockwise direction. Starting from here at the Administration Building, and taking them up to the library first. Straight across to our left. I'll go the other way, starting with the Student Centre - that round building over there...

Linda:　Fine. So, where do I go after the library?

Ross:　I'll show you on this map. Now, the most important thing is that we've got to get back here within an hour. It's 8 o'clock now, the students are getting here at 8.30, so we'll start then and aim to finish the tour at 9.30. If we don't, they'll be late for the photo session. You know, for the student cards ...

Linda:　OK, so I'll keep an eye on my watch as I go ...

Ross:　Good idea. Spend about 10 minutes at the library. Leave at 8.40. Then take them across to the Law Faculty and round to the Economics Block - you should be there by about a quarter to nine. Then on up to the School of Medicine - don't worry about going into the Nursing Block behind it - you won't have time. Now, when you get to the Humanities Block A - at the top left - it'll be about 5 to 9, I suppose. Show them the Halls of Residence next, that's important, then on down to Humanities Block B. Make sure you leave there by about 10 past, won't you?

Linda:　I hope they don't mind walking ...

Ross:　Oh, it'll be good exercise for them. Now, go around the bottom end of the football oval, and on up to the School of Fashion and Textiles. Spend about 10 minutes there because most of your group of students will have enrolled at that school ...

Linda:　So, I'll leave there at about twenty five past ... just let me write that down ...

Ross:　Yeah, and then walk past the Science Theatre, you won't have time to go inside, and come down round the back of the Environmental Sciences Block, and keep going until you get to the Sports Centre. Show them the tennis courts on your ... er ... left as you come down ...

Linda:　Hey, I'm not going to make it back to the Admin Building by half past nine, am I?

Ross:　No, but that's alright. The student card photo session is taking place in the Sports Centre this semester. They're painting the inside of the Administration Building this week. Anyway, I'll hurry my group along and get back first. By the time my students have their student cards, you'll be ready and waiting.

Linda:　Oh. OK. So I'll be at the Sports Centre by ...

Ross:　Well, let's say ... er ... 9.40 at the latest. The only thing you won't have shown them is the Student Centre. But that doesn't matter. You can do that after they've got their student cards. Any questions?

Linda:　No. Everything seems fine.

Ross:　Good. Come on. Let's get a coffee before they start arriving.

ANSWER KEY

◫ LISTENING ANSWERS 1.4 - 1.9 *(pages 6 - 7)*

1.4 (1) games   (2) research   (3) react   (4) violent   (5) sells
      (6) females / female players (gamers)   (7) software   (8) interactive   (9) frustrations   (10) 01256-381574

1.5 (i) b   (ii) b   (iii) d   (iv) a

1.6 **Radio Item 1:**
    i.   some social commentators
    ii. (video games) with extreme content
    iii. rely more on discovery and the development of relationships between the characters onscreen
    iv. stereotyping
    v. higher scores and faster music

    Radio Item 2:
    i.   Ordinary magazines sometimes make a good profit, and sometimes they do not.
    ii. It is a replica (though obviously not <u>exactly</u> the same) of other desk-topped magazines whose ideas and production methods have been copied.
    iii. 2300   iv. Design College   v. (it) tells it like it is / doesn't leave out any facts / doesn't tell lies

1.8 a. T   b. T   c. F   d. T   e. T   f. F   g. NG   h. T   i. F   j. F

1.9 (Maximum four word answers only)
    i. linguists   ii. 1. while asleep   2. while driving a car   iii. words spoken to them
    iv. 760 (words)   v. they think differently / think in different ways

◫ READING ANSWERS 1.2 - 1.11 *(pages 8 - 12)*

1.2 1. How would you describe the shape of the Sydney Opera House?
     2. How and when was the design of the Opera House chosen?

1.4 Paragraphs 1 & 2:
    i. graceful   ii. heated   iii. bustle   iv. abiding   v. distinctive   vi. (to) forge
    vii. striving   viii. brashness

    Paragraphs 3 & 4:
    i. intended   ii. interfered   iii. scaled down   iv. restricted   v. hailed
    vi. appreciably   vii. (to) vow   viii. petty   ix. acclaim   x. budget

1.5 i. c   ii. a   iii. d
    iv.   a) the Opera House
         b) all Australians
         c) the State Government's interference / concerns about the cost *(both answers are possible)*
         d) rehearsal rooms and other facilities (for the various theatres within the complex)

1.6 (1) modern   (2) 1975   (3) distinctive   (4) architect   (5) interior
    (6) 14   (7) controversy   (8) acclaimed   (9) masterpiece   (10) artists

1.7 i. famous design (Pattern Type 2)   v. original specifications (Pattern Type 2)
    ii. heated discussion (Pattern Type 3)   vi. restricted budget (Pattern Type 1)
    iii. set amidst (Pattern Type 2)   vii. petty squabbling (Pattern Type 2)
    iv. tough world (Pattern Type 2)

1.8 a. (l)   b. (m)   c. (h)   d. (j)   e. (o)   f. (p)

1.9 a. T   b. T   c. NG   d. F   e. F   f. T   g. NG   h. F   i. NG   j. NG

1.10 i.   1. sails of a sailing ship   2. broken eggshells *(in either order)*
     ii. (the building) first put the country (firmly) on the world cultural map
     iii. international competition *(2 words maximum)*
     iv. the State Government interfered with Utzon's plans / concerns about the cost
     v. Rehearsal rooms and other facilities (for the various theatres within the complex)
     vi. curved, twisted

1.11 **Across:**
    1. cultural   6. area   7. none   8. petty   9. round   11. are   13. suspicious
    14. paint   15. star   17. (to) ebb   19. theory   20. time   21. year
    23. multi   26. (to) interfere   27. reduced   28. theatre
    Down:
    1. controversy   2. linguist   3. (to) let   4. (to) say   5. range   10. architecture
    12. lottery   16. amidst   18. 'bye   22. rapid   23. mere   24. led   25. inch

✍ WRITING ANSWERS 1.1 - 1.7 *(pages 13 - 16)*

1.1   (1) 1998   (2) 1249   (3) 194   (4) 31   (5) 122   (6) 82   (7) 33   (8) 3134
      (9) 1474   (10) 405   (11) 204   (12) 1051   (13) 1696   (14) 332   (15) 44   (16) 29
      (17) 151   (18) 1287   (19) 76   (20) 942

      (i) c   (ii) a   (iii) b   (iv) e   (v) d

MODEL ANSWER:

The table shows the sales figures of fiction books, non-fiction books, and magazines in a college bookshop for February 2000. The figures <u>are divided</u> into two groups: sales to non–Book Club members and to Book Club members.

The non–Book Club member figures comprise sales to college staff, college students, and members of the public. College staff bought 332 magazines, 44 fiction and 29 non-fiction books. College students bought 1249 magazines, 194 non-fiction and 31 fiction books. More magazines <u>were sold</u> to college students than to any other group of customers. Although no fiction books <u>were sold</u> to members of the public, they purchased 122 non-fiction books and 82 magazines.

Book Club members bought more fiction (76) and non-fiction books (942) than other customers. On the other hand, magazine sales to Club members (33) were fewer than for any other type of customer.

The total number of publications sold for the month was 3134 (1474 to college students, 405 to staff, 204 to the public, and 1051 to Book Club members). Of this figure, 151 items were fiction books and 1287 were non-fiction. Therefore, magazines accounted for the greatest number of sales (1696).   **(194 words)**

1.2   There are 3 instances of the passive voice in the model answer (underlined above). The first is in the **present** because it refers to the way in which the figures about the sales are currently being described, and two are in the **past** because they refer to the situation when the sales were actually made.

    a.   Figures for both male and females <u>are given</u> by the data in the graph.
    b.   Information regarding TV sales to various age-groups <u>is shown</u> in the table.
    c.   Data on radio listeners <u>are included</u> (<u>displayed</u>) (by the statistics) in the bar chart.
    d.   Figures for the rate of vocabulary acquisition at various ages <u>are denoted</u> in the chart.
    e.   The diagram <u>is divided</u> into four sections, one for each language.
    f.   The CD <u>is placed</u> (by the user) into the CD-ROM and the program <u>is loaded</u> into memory.
    g.   2000 CDs <u>were sold</u> (by the music store) in the month of May to persons aged 20-25.

1.3   a.   Topic: Various methods of learning a foreign language.
           Topic Question: Are (they) successful?
      b.   Topic: Television (-viewing).
           Topic Question: Does (it) have a negative effect on society?
      c.   Topic: The Arts.
           Topic Question: Should (they) be better funded by the government? / Should there be more control over where the money goes?

1.4   (1) therefore   (2) however / (but)   (3) in the first place   (4) although / (even though)
      (5) secondly / (furthermore)   (6) however   (7) also / (in the first place)   (8) furthermore / (secondly)
      (9) not only   (10) but   (11) in general   (12) even though / (although)

1.5   (1) a   (2) a   (3) -   (4) a   (5) -   (6) a   (7) -   (8) the
      (9) a   (10) -   (11) the   (12) -   (13) a   (14) a   (15) -   (16) -
      (17) -   (18) -   (19) -   (20) the   (21) a   (22) the   (23) -   (24) an
      (25) -   (26) a   (27) -   (28) -   (29) a   (30) -

1.6   a.   There are obvious advantages of learning English in Britain.
      b.   Students can experience the culture first-hand which is a great help when trying to understand the language.
      c.   If students attend a language school full-time the teachers will be native-speakers.
      d.   It is preferable to study English in an English-speaking country.
      e.   A reasonable level of English can be achieved in one's own country, if a student is gifted and dedicated to study.

1.7   a.   (1) of   (2) of
      b.   (3) at   (4) to   (5) about   (6) for   (7) to   (8) in
      c.   (9) of / to   (10) in   (11) to   (12) to / -   (13) to / with
      d.   (14) to   (15) with   (16) for
      (Check the model answer on page 15 for correct punctuation of the sentences.)

SPELLING ANSWERS 1.1 - 1.4 *(page 17)*

1.1	a. 2	b. 1	c. 3
1.2	a. 6	b. 4	c. 5
1.3	a. 7	b. 9	c. 8
1.4	a. 12	b. 13	c. 11	d. 10

SPELLING RULE EXCEPTIONS:

Rule 1.   'Likable' and 'likeable' are accepted spellings.

Rule 2.   With 'able' / 'ible' the 'e' is dropped in the adverb form   e.g. sensible - sensibly etc.
          Also, note the following exceptions: true - truly / due - duly / argue / argument

Rule 8.   Exceptions: day + ly = daily / gay + ly = gaily

Rule 9.   The more common exceptions are: eight / either / foreign / height / leisure / neighbour / neither / seize / their / weight

Rule 12.   Note that when 'ly' is added to the suffix 'ful' to form an adverb, the 'l' is doubled.

GRAMMAR ANSWERS 1.1 - 1.4 *(pages 18 - 20)*

1.1

1. difficult - **adjective**
2. precisely - **adverb**
3. word - **noun**
4. almost - **adverb**
5. with - **preposition**
6. customary - **adjective**
7. considered - **past participle**
8. that - **pronoun**
9. background - **noun**
10. the - **definite article**
11. determines - **verb**
12. it - **pronoun**
13. various - **adjective**
14. although - **conjunction**
15. membership - **noun**
16. perhaps - **adverb**
17. even- **adverb**
18. extreme - **adjective**
19. between - **preposition**
20. and - **conjunction**
21. make up - **phrasal verb**
22. acceptable - **adjective**
23. closer - **adjective**
24. us - **pronoun**
25. a - **indefinite article**
26. apparent - **adjective**
27. we - **pronoun**
28. its - **possessive pronoun**
29. analysing - **gerund**
30. beginning - **present participle**

1.2   a. complete / b. incomplete / c. complete / d. incomplete / e. complete / f. incomplete / g. incomplete / h. complete / i. incomplete / j. complete / k. incomplete / l. incomplete / m. complete / n. incomplete

1.3   a. The pen and the paper **are** on the desk. / b. The box of chocolates **is** on the shelf. / c. Every one of the students **has** practised very hard. / d. correct / e. correct / f. The number of people who are mobile phone owners **rises** every year. / g. It used to be thought that learning languages **wastes** time. / h. correct / i. She is taking the test twice because she **believes** it is best to have a trial run. / j. In the '50s, the comedy team of Abbott and Costello **was** world famous. / k. Every day there is another driver who **loses** his driving licence due to speed. / l. None of the students **sits** at the back of the lecture theatre. / m. No-one **knows** exactly why economics **is** more important now than in the past. / n. Neither of the debates **was** successful.

1.4

i. d	ii. c	iii. d	iv. d	v. b	vi. a
vii. d	viii. b	ix. c	x. d	xi. b	xii. d

VOCABULARY ANSWERS 1.3 *(page 21)*

1.3

Place	Person	Gerund/Thing	Adjective	Verb	Adverb
-	writer	writing	written *	write	-
-	designer	designing/design/designation	designing *	design	-
art gallery	artist	art	artistic	-	artistically
-	communicator	communicating/communication	communicative *	communicate	communicatively
-	-	expression	expressive *	express	expressively
-	-	meaning	meaningful	mean	meaningfully
information desk	informant	informing/information	informative *	inform	informatively
-	-	explanation	explanatory *	explain	-
-	-	conclusion	conclusive *	conclude	conclusively
development	developer	developing/development	developing *	develop	-
-	-	encouragement	encouraging	encourage	encouragingly

NB: The given words in the exercise are underlined.

* past participles (and '-ing' forms) may also be adjectival in some cases i.e. *a written document* (designed / communicated / expressed / informed / explained / concluded / developed)

◼ LISTENING ANSWERS 2.4 - 2.9 *(pages 23 - 24)*

2.4 (1) ice (2) fresh (3) farming (4) sewage (5) developing
(6) disease (7) polluted (8) 35,000 (9) tables (10) 0171-825-992

2.5 (i) d (ii) b (iii) d (iv) a

2.6 **Radio Item 3:**
i. 'Planet Watch'
ii. it is scattered unevenly (about the globe)
iii. less than 5%
iv. reservoirs
v. they depend on wet areas (that are fast drying up)

Radio Item 4:
i. approximately 200 metres offshore
ii. the resort and tourism
iii. fish / catch fish / bathe / swim
iv. (fore)shorten the 2 kilometre long rock shelf
v. slight changes in the recent patterns of (moon) tides

2.8 a. T b. T c. NG d. T e. NG f. F g. F h. T i. NG j. T

2.9 *(Maximum four word answers only)*
i. agricultural and industrial excesses ii. (the) World Wildlife Fund
iii. change in political thinking iv. greed v. (more) efficient energy sources

◼ READING ANSWERS 2.2 - 2.11 *(pages 25 - 29)*

2.2 1. Is it possible that a species can adapt to changes in the environment?
2. Do you know what the ozone layer protects the earth from?

2.4 Paragraphs 1 & 2:
i. teeming ii. unsettling iii. inadvertently iv. demise v. decline vi. ecology
Paragraphs 3 & 4:
i. extinct ii. phenomenon iii. contributory iv. contemporaries v. bizarre vi. (to) shield

2.5 i. Paragraph 1 - d Paragraph 2 - a Paragraph 3 - f Paragraph 4 - e
ii. c iii. a) a frog b) amphibians c) frogs of the species *Rana klepton esculenta*
d) the unusual bi and (even) tri-coloured frogs

2.6 Parts of speech: (1) verb form (-ing) (2) noun (3) verb (4) adjective (5) noun
(6) verb form (-ing) (7) noun (8) adjective (9) noun (10) adjective

(1) warning (2) disaster (3) reverse (4) difficult (5) development
(6) disappearing (7) rainforest (8) sensitive (9) variations (10) environmental

2.7 i. all over the world (Pattern Type 3) ii. at a loss (Pattern Type 3)
iii. amphibian species (Pattern Type 1) iv. all manner of wildlife (Pattern Type 2)
v. bizarre (Pattern Type 3) vi. put forward (Pattern Type 3)
vii. fit the facts (Pattern Type 3)

2.9 a. F b. F c. T d. T e. NG f. T g. T h. NG i. F j. T k. F

2.10 i. city / wet areas / all over the world / remote jungles *(any 3 answers only)*
ii. 1. we may lose a vital link in the ecological chain / an increase in pestilent insects
2. we might be increasing our output of air pollutants to irreversible levels
iii. lighter coloured skins iv. ozone layer depletion v. 4

2.11 **Across:**
1. ecosystem 5. (to) fit 8. unspoilt 9. flat 10. wet 13. toad 16. nose
17. sewage 19. re 20. irreversible 21. at 23. part 25. remote
27. endanger 30. not 33. blast 35. turbine 38. tide
Down:
2. sensitive 3. moon 4. kit 5. (to) flow 6. of 7. catastrophe 11. tree
12. environment 14. as 15. demise 18. great 22. ten 24. trap 2. rigs
26. on 28. rely 29. gas 31. out 32. tri 34. two 36. BD 37. i.e.

◼ WRITING ANSWERS 2.2 - 2.8 *(pages 30 - 35)*

2.2 (1) cyclist (2) is balanced (3) seat (4) saddle (5) handles / handlebars (6) pedals
(7) notched cog (8) is connected / is linked (9) metal chain (10) wheel hub (11) gear lever
(12) brake lever (13) is connected / is linked (14) cable (15) set of brakes (16) air pump
(17) rubber tyres (18) are filled (19) speedometer (20) headlamp

MODEL ANSWER:

A bicycle is a machine designed to transport a person by means of his or her own physical effort. It is, therefore, almost entirely environmentally-friendly. Since the amount of friction generated is much reduced, it is also extremely efficient.

It consists of four main sections: the two spoked wheels, a set of handlebars, and a revolving cog, held together by a metal frame. The cyclist, who is balanced on top of a seat covered by a soft saddle, leans forwards and grips the handlebars, pushing down with his or her feet on the pedals which rotate up and down. They drive a central notched cog which is connected by a metal chain to the back wheel hub. Alternative gear positions are available by operating a gear lever at hand level. Also on the handlebars is the brake lever, which is linked by a cable to a set of brakes on the back wheel.

Accessories include an air pump, with which the rubber tyres are filled periodically with air, a speedometer, and a headlamp for use at night.

(177 words)

2.4   a.   Topic: Recycling domestic waste.
            Topic Question: Is (it) beneficial? How can a householder help to conserve valuable resources?
       b.   Topic: Public transport and private car ownership.
            Topic Question: Should the government spend more on (the former) and discourage (the latter) to reduce air pollution in major cities?
       c.   Topic: Smoking in public places.
            Topic Question: Should (it) be allowed? / What rights do smokers have?

2.5   (1) in addition / (also) / (moreover)   (2) too / (also)   (3) and   (4) also
      (5) moreover / (in addition) / (also)   (6) firstly   (7) secondly / (moreover) / (in addition)
      (8) but   (9) eventually (10) also   (11) for example   (12) to sum up   (13) and

2.6   (1) -   (2) the   (3) the   (4) the /-   (5) -   (6) a   (7) -   (8) the /-
      (9) -   (10) the / an   (11) the / -   (12) the   (13) the   (14) -   (15) the   (16) -
      (17) the   (18) -   (19) -   (20) -   (21) an   (22) the   (23) an   (24) the
      (25) -   (26) -   (27) -

2.7   a.   In poor countries it is difficult to provide enough food to feed even the present number of people.
       b.   In China couples are punished financially if they have more than one child.
       c.   In rich, industrialised and developing countries it is very difficult for governments to provide effective public services in overcrowded cities.
       d.   Further large increases in population only cause more overcrowding, unemployment and crime.

2.8   a.   (1) in   (2) to
       b.   (3) to   (4) of   (5) to   (6) of   (7) in   (8) to / and
       c.   (9) of   (10) of / from   (11) in   (12) in   (13) in / of
(Check the completed model answer on page 34 for correct punctuation of the sentences.)

❋ SPELLING ANSWERS 2.1 - 2.2 *(page 36)*

2.1   a.   studying / language / country / where / widely / spoken / many / advantages
       b.   overseas / students / learn / English / comprehensive / school / university / nowadays
       c.   their / knowledge / grammar / often / quite / advanced / which / certainly / useful foreigners / live / English-speaking / environment
       d.   Britain / there / opportunities / practise / listening / speaking / English
       e.   preferable / make / friends / native / speaker / order / practise / conversation
       f.   reasonable / level / achieved / quickly / student / dedicated / study

2.2   abbreviation / accomplish / acquisition / adaptation / administration / analysis / approach / appropriate assignment / bibliography / chronological / classify / campus / communication / comparatively / comprehensive comprise / context / correspond / counsellor (or councillor) / curriculum / diploma / discussion / economic eligible / enrolment / essential / evaluate / evidence / facility / foundation / generally / improvise / inadequate

❋ GRAMMAR ANSWERS 2.1 - 2.7 *(pages 37 - 39)*

2.1 A

affect	affected	affected	educate	educated	educated	help	helped	helped
believe	believed	believed	enjoy	enjoyed	enjoyed	join	joined	joined
climb	climbed	climbed	escape	escaped	escaped	kick	kicked	kicked
connect	connected	connected	flow	flowed	flowed	submit	submitted	submitted
drop	dropped	dropped	happen	happened	happened	wait	waited	waited

B

be	was	been	go	went	gone	speak	spoke	spoken
bring	brought	brought	have	had	had	shrink	shrank	shrank
drive	drove	driven	sleep	slept	slept	teach	taught	taught
eat	ate	eaten	shoot	shot	shot	think	thought	thought
fly	flew	flown	strike	struck	struck	write	wrote	wrote

C

buy	bought	bought	feel	felt	felt	put	put	put
catch	caught	caught	find	found	found	spring	sprang	sprung
cut	cut	cut	meet	met	met	swim	swam	swum
cost	cost	cost	ran	ran	run	wake	woke	woke
draw	drew	drawn	sit	sat	sat	wind	wound	wound

D

awake	awoke	awaken	flew	fled	flown	make	made	made
do	did	done	forecast	forecasted	forecasted	ring	rang	rung
dream	dreamt *	dreamt *	hang	hung **	hung **	spoil	spoilt***	spoilt***
fall	fell	fallen	hear	heard	heard	swing	swung	swung
fight	fought	fought	know	knew	known	weep	wept	wept

    * or dreamed   ** or hang/hanged/hanged (alternative meaning)   *** or spoiled

2.2
i.   saw // helped / helps / has helped / had helped
ii. have lived // think
iii. is / was   iv. was / own   v.   introduce // provide // continue
vi. fail // bring about   vii. was not / has not been   viii. compromise // do not want
ix. is   x. increased

2.3

Zero:	If + **present**	**simple** / **continuous**	tense … , + present simple tense …	+ infinitive …
1st:	If + **present**	**simple** / **continuous**	tense … , + **will/may/might/ can/must/should** …	+ infinitive …
2nd:	If + **past**	**simple** / **continuous**	tense … , + **would/might/could etc.** …	+ infinitive …
3rd:	If + **past perfect tense**		… , + **would might could** have	… + **past participle** …

2.4
i. 1st   ii. 2nd   iii. 1st   iv. 1st   v. 1st   vi. mixed   vii. 1st   viii. zero
ix. 3rd   x. 2nd   xi. mixed   xii. 1st

2.5
i. was   ii. is   iii. are/are/those/lives   iv. uses/is   v. was   vi. was/was   vii. are

2.6

line 1	Australian / the Sydney Morning Herald / Tuesday / May		
lines 2 & 3	Sydney's / the University of Sydney	*line 11*	the Authority
line 5	Dr. Michael Dawson / Dr. Brent Young	*line 12*	the NSW Roads and Traffic Authority
line 6	Chemistry Department / Britain	*line 13*	Sydney's
lines 7 & 8	Mr. Noel Child / Sydney's	*line 14*	International Environment Association / July
line 9	the New South Wales Environment Protection Authority		

2.7
it	*(line 1)*	- 'the entire ecological system on earth'
that/their	*(line 2)*	- 'an infinitesimal number of interconnecting parts'
this	*(line 4)*	- 'the entire ecological system on earth … functioning of the whole'
doing so	*(line 5)*	- 'forget(ting) we are inextricably linked to nature'
its	*(line 5)*	- 'nature' (or 'the entire ecological system on earth')
those/their	*(line 7)*	- (persons) 'who ignore nature's warnings'
these	*(line 8)*	- (politicians) 'who ignore nature's warnings'
they	*(line 10)*	- '(these) politicians' or 'politicians … who ignore nature's warnings'
this	*(line 10)*	- 'ceas(ing) to be respected'
them	*(line 11)*	- 'our very systems of government' or 'these politicians'

★ VOCABULARY ANSWERS 2.1 - 2.3 *(page 40)*

2.1

Noun Indicators							Adjective Indicators				
-er	-ism	-ist	-ment	-ness	-tion	-ship	-al	-ish	-ous	-ive	-ic
Verb Indicators							**Adverb Indicators**				
-fy	-ise (-ize)	-ate					-ly				

2.3

Place	Person	Gerund/Thing	Adjective	Verb	Adverb
-	polluter	polluting/pollution	polluted *	pollute-	
environment	environmentalist	-	environmental	-	environmentally
-	destroyer	destroying/destruction	destructive *	destroy	destructively
-	-	preventing/prevention	preventive **	prevent	preventively
conservatory	conservationist	conserving/conservation	conservative *	conserve	conservatively
-	protector	protecting/protection	protective *	protect	protectively
penal institution	-	penalty	penal	penalise	-
disaster area	-	disaster	disastrous	-	disastrously
-	-	varying/variety	various *	vary	variously
nature	naturalist/native	-	natural/native	-	naturally
-	-	specifying/species	specific *	specify	specifically

NB: The given words in the exercise are underlined.   ** also 'preventative'
* past participles (and '-ing' forms) may also be adjectival in some cases i.e. *a polluted country* (destroyed / prevented / conserved / protected / varied / specified)

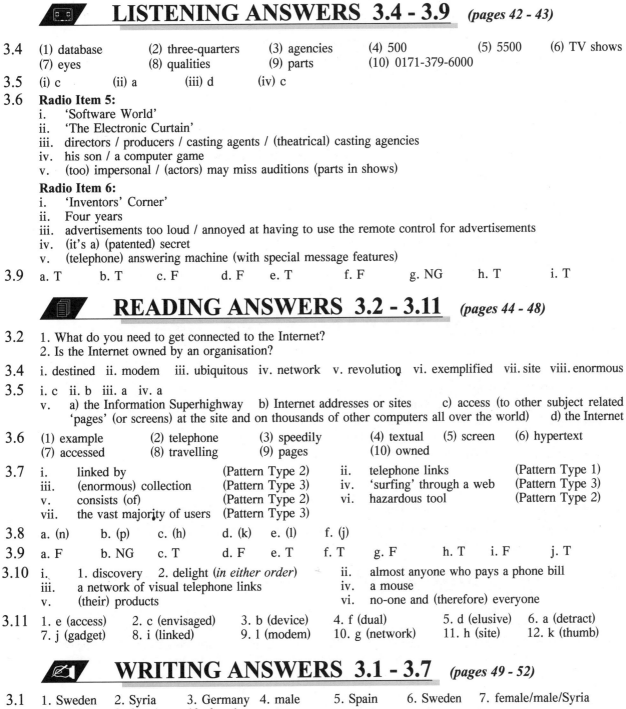

LISTENING ANSWERS 3.4 - 3.9 *(pages 42 - 43)*

3.4   (1) database   (2) three-quarters   (3) agencies   (4) 500   (5) 5500   (6) TV shows
      (7) eyes   (8) qualities   (9) parts   (10) 0171-379-6000

3.5   (i) c   (ii) a   (iii) d   (iv) c

3.6   **Radio Item 5:**
      i.   'Software World'
      ii.   'The Electronic Curtain'
      iii.   directors / producers / casting agents / (theatrical) casting agencies
      iv.   his son / a computer game
      v.   (too) impersonal / (actors) may miss auditions (parts in shows)

      Radio Item 6:
      i.   'Inventors' Corner'
      ii.   Four years
      iii.   advertisements too loud / annoyed at having to use the remote control for advertisements
      iv.   (it's a) (patented) secret
      v.   (telephone) answering machine (with special message features)

3.9   a. T   b. T   c. F   d. F   e. T   f. F   g. NG   h. T   i. T

READING ANSWERS 3.2 - 3.11 *(pages 44 - 48)*

3.2   1. What do you need to get connected to the Internet?
      2. Is the Internet owned by an organisation?

3.4   i. destined   ii. modem   iii. ubiquitous   iv. network   v. revolution   vi. exemplified   vii. site   viii. enormous

3.5   i. c   ii. b   iii. a   iv. a
      v.   a) the Information Superhighway   b) Internet addresses or sites   c) access (to other subject related
         'pages' (or screens) at the site and on thousands of other computers all over the world)   d) the Internet

3.6   (1) example   (2) telephone   (3) speedily   (4) textual   (5) screen   (6) hypertext
      (7) accessed   (8) travelling   (9) pages   (10) owned

3.7   i.   linked by   (Pattern Type 2)   ii.   telephone links   (Pattern Type 1)
      iii.   (enormous) collection   (Pattern Type 3)   iv.   'surfing' through a web   (Pattern Type 3)
      v.   consists (of)   (Pattern Type 2)   vi.   hazardous tool   (Pattern Type 2)
      vii.   the vast majority of users   (Pattern Type 3)

3.8   a. (n)   b. (p)   c. (h)   d. (k)   e. (l)   f. (j)

3.9   a. F   b. NG   c. T   d. F   e. T   f. T   g. F   h. T   i. F   j. T

3.10   i.   1. discovery   2. delight (*in either order*)   ii.   almost anyone who pays a phone bill
       iii.   a network of visual telephone links   iv.   a mouse
       v.   (their) products   vi.   no-one and (therefore) everyone

3.11   1. e (access)   2. c (envisaged)   3. b (device)   4. f (dual)   5. d (elusive)   6. a (detract)
      7. j (gadget)   8. i (linked)   9. l (modem)   10. g (network)   11. h (site)   12. k (thumb)

WRITING ANSWERS 3.1 - 3.7 *(pages 49 - 52)*

3.1   1. Sweden   2. Syria   3. Germany   4. male   5. Spain   6. Sweden   7. female/male/Syria
      8. CAD   9. female   10. female

3.2   (1) 17   (2) 5   (3) 3   (4) 1   (5) 9   (6) 7   (7) 6   (8) 4
      (9) 1   (10) 2   (11) 21   (12) 9   (13) 12   (14) 11
      i) a   ii) e   iii) d   iv) c   v) b

MODEL ANSWER:

According to the bar chart, students from four European countries (Sweden, Spain, France and Germany) and one Middle Eastern country (Syria) are taking Graphic Design at the college. Some students are enrolled in the Computer-Aided Design (CAD) core option; the others are taking Photography.

Overall, Sweden has the largest number of enrolled students (17) and Syria the smallest (5). France and Spain both have 12 students; Germany has 11. It is noticeable that France and Germany have similar profiles.

Students from all five countries are enrolled in CAD, but more males are taking this option than females (21 and 9 respectively). For each nationality the males taking CAD outnumber the females, except in the case of the Syrians with 3 females to only 1 male. Sweden has the most students studying CAD (9); Spain is next with 7, while France has 6. Germany and Syria have 4 CAD students each.

As for the photography option, more females than males are enrolled from every country except Syria. In fact, no female Syrian students are taking Photographic Design. Only 1 male from each country is enrolled in Photography, except for 2 males from Spain.   **(192 words)**

3.3   a.   Topic: Computers (in the office)
           Topic Question: What are the advantages and disadvantages of relying on (them) to run a small business?
     b.   Topic: Medical technology increasing natural life-span.
           Topic Question: What are the possible effects of (it)?
     c.   Topic: Owning a mobile phone.
           Topic Question: What are the pros and cons of (it)?

3.4   (See the model answer on page 52 for the introduction.)

3.5   a. (1) -   (2) an   (3) -   (4) - / the   (5) -   (6) the   (7) - / the   (8) -   (9) -   (10) the   (11) a   (12) -
     b. (13) -   (14) -   (15) -   (16) -   (17) the   (18) - / the   (19) a   (20) the   (21) - / the

     c. The main topic idea is: The use of nuclear technology for military purposes.

       The supporting arguments are: 1. Enough bombs have been built to destroy the Earth.   2. One day some country may start a nuclear war.   3. Too many countries now have the technology to make nuclear bombs.

       The summary statement begins: '... there is much current debate ...'

3.6   (See the model answer on page 52 for the conclusion.)

3.7   (1) although / (though) / (even though)   (2) however
     (3) even though / (although) /(though)   (4) such as   (5) such as   (6) however
     (7) and   (8) and / (but)   (9) though / (however)   (10) and / (but)
     (11) and   (12) in conclusion   (13) but   (14) however

✹ SPELLING ANSWERS 3.1 - 3.2   *(page 53)*

3.1   c. repetitive
     g. technologies / resources
     a. of / appliances / purchase
     f. recorders / suitable / based / preference
     j. others / thoroughly / statistically / producing / than
     h. heaters / drawing / monitors / minimise / consumption / automatically
     e. also / garage / doors / telephones / divert / preset / destinations
     i. naturally / these / new / their / detractors / usually / margin / error
     d. example / digital / invoked / for / session / used / to / personal / favourites
     b. transistorised / computer / chips / determine / our / preferences / various / machines / microwaves / television

3.2   innovative / irrelevant / laboratory / literally / illogical / material / media / minimum / noticeable / percentage / persuade / postgraduate / postpone / preference / process / programme

✹ GRAMMAR ANSWERS 3.1 - 3.5   *(pages 54 - 55)*

3.1   i. non-defining   ii. defining   iii. defining   iv. defining   v. non-defining   vi. non-defining
     (Unlike defining clauses, non-defining clauses are separated from the main clause by commas.)

3.3   i. who is technologically ignorant   ii. that are farmed for food   iii. who are proficient with computers
     iv. which are manufactured in countries employing cheap labour   v. that refuse to read the fine print

3.5   i. was   ii. is   iii. is   iv. is   v. determines / receive   vi. requires / its   vii. know

✪ VOCABULARY ANSWERS 3.1   *(page 59)*

3.1

Place	Person	Gerund/Thing	Adjective	Verb	Adverb
-	technician	technology	technical	-	technically
(factory)	manufacturer	manufacturing/manufacture	manufactured *	manufacture	-
-	-	computing/computer/computation	computerised *	compute	-
network	networker	networking	networked *	network	-
-	-	televising/television	televisual *	televise	-
-	inventor	inventing/invention	inventive *	invent	-
-	discoverer	discovering/discovery	discovered *	discover	-
-	importer	importing/import	imported *	import	-
-		effect	effective	-	effectively
construction	constructor	constructing/construction	constructive *	construct	constructively
-	-	evolving/evolution	evolved *	evolve	

NB: The given words in the exercise are underlined.

* past participles (and '-ing' forms) may also be adjectival in some cases i.e. *a manufactured item* (computerised / networked / televised / invented / discovered / imported / constructed / evolved)

🔊 LISTENING ANSWERS 4.4 - 4.9 *(pages 61 - 62)*

4.4 (1) university   (2) city / poor   (3) English   (4) funding   (5) longer   (6) upward
(7) older   (8) Britain / this country   (9) 50,000   (10) 0171-389-4204

4.5 **Radio Item 7:**
i.   non-English-speaking persons have immigrated to Britain
ii.   the value of bringing non-English-speaking immigrants to this country in the future
iii.   the press
iv.   The percentage (of funding for English courses) has significantly increased
v.   i.   the (total) number of immigrants (to Britain) is (a mere) 50,000 a year
ii.   that (number) includes many who speak English well

4.6 **Radio Item 8:**
Diagram A best describes the situation heard on tape.
i.   December 1st   ii.   to offset the (increased educational) cost ... of (recent) computer purchases in primary
schools   iii.   beer manufacturers   iv. 20% rise in the cost of a packet of cigarettes

4.9 a. T   b. T   c. T   d. F   e. T   f. F   g. NG   h. F   i. T   j. NG

📄 READING ANSWERS 4.2 - 4.11 *(pages 63 - 67)*

4.2 1. Which political party in Britain (and Europe) is concerned with environmental issues?
2. Do you know the names of other parties in the country in which you are studying?

4.4 i. dominated (by)   ii. agendas   iii. (to) safeguard   iv. perplexed   v. faithful   vi. comparatively
vii. (to) implement   viii. equitable

4.5 i. b   ii. c   iii. a   iv. c   v. a) one of the two parties that a British voter leans towards supporting b) a fair division
of wealth in the country   c) wealth   d) less attention ... is paid to the smaller parties

4.6 (1) control   (2) recently   (3) loyal   (4) Labour   (5) unions   (6) society
(7) Conservative   (8) freedom   (9) attention   (10) current

4.7 i.   to tell apart   (Pattern Type 3)   ii.   lean towards   (Pattern Type 2)
iii.   strong connections with   (Pattern Type 2)   iv.   population base   (Pattern Type 1)
v.   the concept of   (Pattern Type 2)   vi.   assisted in their quest for   (Pattern Type 3)
vii.   kept in check   (Pattern Type 3)

4.8 a. (i)   b. (l)   c. (j)   d. (k)   e. (m)   f. (n)

4.9 a. T   b. NG   c. NG   d. F   e. NG   f. F   g. T   h. T   i. NG   j. F

4.10 i.   1. the common working man   2. the trade unions   *(in either order)*
ii.   (there is a) smaller taxpaying population base   iii.   government spending
iv.   the less politically powerful   v.   one major current issue   vi.   4

4.11 1. e (attention)   2. d (base)   3. a (wealth)   4. c (loyal)   5. b (quest)   6. f (freedom)
7. j (trade)   8. h (migrants)   9. l (federal)   10. i (solely)   11. g (dominated)   12. k (myth)

✍ WRITING ANSWERS 4.1 - 4.5 *(pages 68 - 71)*

4.1 1. Acme Sports Cars 2. Branson Motors 3. Acme Sports Cars 4. July to September '99   5. August and
September '99 6. October and December '99   7. Acme Sports Cars   8. £80,000 (at the end of June '99)

4.2 (1) £70,000   (2) £60,000   (3) £80,000   (4) £80,000   (5) £10,000   (6) £60,000
(7) £40,000   (8) £60,000   (9) £20,000   (10) £60,000   (11) £40,000   (12) £20,000
(13) £40,000   (14) 2000   (15) 12
(i) c   (ii) d   (iii) b   (iv) a
(A) decreased slightly   (B) rose sharply   (C) fell dramatically   (D) gradually increased

MODEL ANSWER:

The graph shows the four quarters of the 2000 financial year and the monthly profit of Acme Sports Cars and Branson Motors for 12 months. The former was making almost twice the profit at the beginning than at the end of the financial year. There was a three-fold increase in the latter's monthly profit over the same period.

During the first quarter, Acme Sports Cars' monthly profit decreased slightly from £70,000 to £60,000, but rose sharply to £80,000 by the end of June. Branson Motors' monthly profit, however, doubled from £20,000 to £40,000.

Due to the introduction of a luxury goods tax, Acme Sports Cars' monthly profit fell dramatically during the second quarter from £80,000 to only £10,000, whereas that of Branson Motors continued to rise, peaking at just over £60,000 by the end of September.

In the third quarter, Acme Sports Cars' monthly profit increased steadily to £20,000 and remained stable, while Branson Motors' monthly profits fluctuated between just over £60,000 and £40,000. At the beginning of the last quarter, a boost in the economy meant the monthly profit of both Acme Sports Cars and Branson Motors gradually increased to £40,000 and £60,000 respectively by the financial year's end.   **(200 words)**

4.3 a.   Topic: Stronger gun laws
Topic Question: Should the government introduce (them) to protect all citizens?

b.   Topic: Drinking while driving.
      Topic Question: Is a total ban of (it) the only way to reduce the rising number of road accidents?
c.   Topic: Free speech.
      Topic Question: Is it important to have the right to (it)?

4.4   Essay a. FOR 1, 6, 9 AGAINST 3, 11, 20   Essay b. FOR 12, 15, 18 AGAINST 5, 10
      Essay c. FOR 4, 17, 19 AGAINST 7, 13

4.5   *'Although abuses of the system are inevitable, social welfare payments are essential to*
           protect the rights citizens have to a guaranteed income in a democratic society.' Discuss.

POSSIBLE PLAN

INTRO: = there are abuses of the system
                                    BUT: my opinion = > YES, essential
                        for 2 MAIN REASONS: 1. *Many require welfare*
                                              2. *Crime*
BODY:

PARAGRAPH 1: (YES + WHY)   REASON 1: *Many require welfare*
                           ARGUMENT 1: *Some people are unable to earn a wage*
                              Examples: *Single parent mothers, disabled, sick*
                           ARGUMENT 2: *The unemployed have the right to an
                                        income too - it is not always their fault
                                        - they've probably paid tax all their lives*

PARAGRAPH 2: (YES + WHY)   REASON 2: *Crime*
                           ARGUMENT 1: *Crime increases if people have no means
                                        of support*
                           ARGUMENT 2: *Fighting crime is more expensive than
                                        providing welfare*
                               Example: *The wages of one policeman are 4 or 5
                                         times higher than a 'dole' payment.*
PARAGRAPH 3: (NO)
                             REASON 1: *Payments increase dependency*
                            Refutation: *True, but for the unemployed, usually
                                         only temporary*
                             REASON 2: *Family's responsibility to assist*
                            Refutation: *It is too expensive to look after the
                                         severely disabled*

CONCLUSION: *(YES +*   WHAT IS PROVED: *Welfare payments essential*
               SUMMARY)   Summary: *A caring society must provide for all*

MODEL ANSWER:

Social welfare is an essential element of an advanced society. Good systems are always abused, but that does not mean they are faulty. In my opinion, the two main reasons why welfare payments are necessary are as follows:

First of all, critics forget that there are many forms of welfare besides payments to the unemployed. Their negative opinions harm those who are not capable of earning a wage, such as single-parent mothers, the disabled, and the sick. Moreover, the unemployed have the right to an income, too. They are not always at fault for not having a job, and in most cases the tax they have paid in the past entitles them to assistance.

The second reason is that crime increases when people have no means of support. The desperately poor inevitably turn to crime, which is not only dangerous but costly. Policing the streets is more expensive than providing welfare. A policeman's wage is four or five times higher than a 'dole' payment.

Certain members of society believe that people should look after themselves. They point out that welfare increases dependency on others and destroys dignity. This may be true, but in the case of the unemployed, the relief payments are usually temporary. It is surely the fault of the government if there are long-term unemployed. Welfare critics also believe that it is the responsibility of a victim's family to provide financial assistance. However, it is too expensive to provide complete help for a severely disabled person.

To conclude, it is vital to understand the need for welfare in a modern democratic society. Without welfare payments the poor are destined to become poorer. The first duty of a government is to provide a financial safety net for all disadvantaged persons, and that includes those without work.   (297 words)

PUNCTUATION ANSWERS 4.1 - 4.2 *(page 72)*

4.1 (i) c) 4   (ii) h) 5   (iii) g) 9   (iv) i) 7   (v) a) 2   (vi) e) 8   (vii) d) 3   (viii) b) 1 (ix) f) 6

4.2 (See Reading Passage 4 on page 64)

✳ **SPELLING ANSWERS 4.1 - 4.2** *(page 73)*

4.1 f. opponent
    g. stubbornness / overwhelming
    d. temptation / pressure / pursuing
    a. pity / politicians / abused / profession
    h. obviously / vast / majority / electors / proved
    j. therefore / surprising / self-interested / women / elected / office.
    b. however / noble / ruthlessness / almost / prerequisite / these / days
    k. perhaps / should / quick / to / blame / elected / carry / out
    c. also / more / difficult / than / past / rise / having / independent / fortune
    i. certainly / self-interest / almost / only / criterion / for / choosing / politician / election / day
    l. democracies/people/invariably/governments/deserve/which/of/intelligence/general/public/politicians
    e. public/always/respected/strong/leaders/problem/trying/to/determine/what/actually/constitutes

4.2 qualify / questionnaire / reference / related / relevant / research / revise / sample
    seminar / specialise / summarise / survey / syllabus / technological / tertiary / transfer
    tuition / tutorial / undergraduate / valid / variables / vocabulary

✳ **GRAMMAR ANSWERS 4.1 - 4.10** *(pages 74 - 77)*

4.1 a. The main purpose of government **is** to provide a stable framework of management within which a country **grows*** steadily and can **prosper****.
    b. Most people, however, usually **take** the view that deciding moral issues eventually **becomes*** the government's responsibility.
    c. In other words, the government **is** not only responsible for managing the economy; it **decides*** what a member of society can and cannot **do**** within that society.
    d. A democracy must **allow**** freedom of thought and expression, but this **does** not mean that all ideas and actions can be tolerated; an individual or group of persons who intentionally **violates*** democratic principles must be restrained.
    e. The majority of people **believes*** that governments should set and maintain the moral code within society, but when this **occurs***, personal freedom is put at risk and **loses*** its perceived importance.
    f. It is often difficult for a politician who **argues*** the case for personal freedom when the general public **demands*** a traditional approach to moral issues.
    g. Politicians almost always **take** a pragmatic approach to their work. The ideal politician, however, **does*** not easily compromise his or her principles.

    * 3rd person singular verb agreement with the present simple tense   ** infinitive after a modal verb

4.2 a. (v) The Prime Minister **has delivered** a speech on taxation to Parliament.
    b. (i) A more equitable society **is becoming** increasingly harder to achieve.
    c. (iv) One of the most problematical political issues of recent years, funding for the National Health Service, **has divided** the present government.
    d. (ii) Comprehensive schools **have suffered** recently at the hands of inept politicians too concerned with saving money.
    e. (iii) In modern day societies, banks **have exerted** great control over the country's financial future.

4.3 Note that constructions with other grammatical persons are possible i.e. *he ---- (doing something)* etc.

    A. | **I   ----   (being / doing / having something)** |

        detest / hate / loathe / enjoy / like / love / risk / stop / try

    B. | **I   ----   to (be /do / have something)** |

        hate / loathe / like / love / try / want / wish

4.4 C. | **I am ----   (being / doing / having something)** |

        afraid **of** / angry **at** * / bored **with** / crazy **about** / depressed **about** / disgusted **at** **/ excited **about**
        / experienced **at** / fed up **with** / frightened **of** / frustrated **with** / good **at** / happy **with** / interested **in**
        / keen **on** / sad **about** / scared **of** / sick **of** / terrible **at** / terrified **of** / tired **of** / wary **of** / worried **about**

    D. | **I am ----   to (be /do / have something)** |

        afraid / crazy / delighted / forced / frightened / happy / interested / keen / loathe / obligated / sad / scared

        * but 'angry **with** (something)'   ** but 'disgusted **at/by/with** (something)'

4.5

	can	could	may	might	will	would	shall	should	ought to	must	need	dare
I ----- (do)(something)	✓	✓	✓	✓	✓	✓	✓	✓	✓	✓	~	✓
I ----- not (do)(something)	✓¹	✓	✓	✓	✓	✓	✓	✓	✓²	✓	✓	✓
I ----- (have done)(something)	~	✓	✓	✓	✓	✓	✓	✓	✓	✓	~	~
I ----- not (have done)(something)	~	✓	✓	✓	✓	✓	✓	✓	✓²	✓	~	✓
I ----- to (do)(something)	~	~	~	~	~	~	~	~	✓³	~	✓	✓
I do not ----- to (do)(something)	~	~	~	~	~	~	~	~	~	~	✓	✓
I ----- (be)(something)	✓	✓	✓	✓	✓	✓	✓	✓	✓	✓	~⁴	✓
I ----- not (be)(something)	✓¹	✓	✓	✓	✓	✓	✓	✓	✓²	✓	✓	✓
I ----- (be doing)(something)	✓	✓	✓	✓	✓	✓	✓	✓	✓	✓	~⁴	~
I ----- not (be doing)(something)	✓¹	✓	✓	✓	✓	✓	✓	✓	✓²	✓	✓	~

NB: contractions are to be avoided in formal writing, but not in informal speech.

¹ 'cannot' is preferable to 'can not' ² 'ought $\underline{not}$ to ...' ³ 'ought to do ...' ⁴ but 'need $\underline{to}$ be ...' is possible

4.7 a. (1) could (2) will (3) should b. (4) dare (5) will c. (6) can (7) will
d. (8) should (9) could e. (10) shall (11) will (12) should

4.8
a. **As soon as** the election results came in, it was clear that the public was unhappy with the previous government's performance.
b. **While** voters considered their options, both political parties were busy making even more election promises.
c. **Before** voters go to the polling booth, a government should fully disclose its policies.
d. **When** a politician is proved to be corrupt, there is usually an increase in accountability of all political representatives.
e. **Since** the introduction of tighter tax laws, more money has become available to the government to implement its policies.

(Note that the clauses in $\underline{all}$ the sentences above may be reversed.)

4.9
a. The National Government is responsible for the nation's security, **whereas** local governments are responsible for administration at a much lower level.
b. The trading policies of most EEC countries are similar, **although** they did not always share a common goal.
c. Politicians used to overlook the needs of immigrants to Britain, **despite** the need for improved English training programmes.

(Note that the clauses in only the three sentences above may be reversed.)

d. Major strikes cost the country enormous amounts of money; **however**, they are sometimes necessary to correct imbalances of power between employers and employees.
e. Social security benefits ensure that the disadvantaged do not suffer, **but** abuses of the system invariably occur.

4.10 a. v. b. iv. c. i. d. ii. e. iii

★ VOCABULARY ANSWERS 4.1 *(page 78)*

4.1

Place	Person	Gerund/Thing	Adjective	Verb	Adverb
-	politician	politics	political	politicise	politically
Government House	governor	governing/government	governmental	govern	governmentally
department	-	department	departmental	-	departmentally
-	-	response/responsibility	responsible/responsive	-	responsibly(ively)
-	negotiator	negotiating/negotiation	negotiated *	negotiate	-
meeting place	-	meeting	met *	meet	-
-	-	recommending/recommendation	recommended *	recommend	-
-	-	system	systematic	systematise	systematically
-	producer	producing/product	productive *	produce	productively
-	economist	economy	economical	economise	economically
control room	controller	controlling/control	controlling *	control	-

NB: The given words in the exercise are underlined.

* past participles (and '-ing' forms) may also be adjectival in some cases i.e. *a negotiated agreement* (met / recommended / produced / controlled)

📼 LISTENING ANSWERS 5.2 - 5.8 *(pages 79 - 81)*

5.2   4 1 5 2 3   →   3 2 5 1 4   →   3 2 5 4 1   →   1 3 5 2 4

5.3   a. T   b. T   c. NG   d. F   e. F   f. NG   g. F   h. T

5.5   i. d   ii. c   iii. d   iv. d   v. b

5.6

ic - indirectly contradicted	*ls* - lacking sense	*nm* - not mentioned	*dc* - directly contradicted

   i.   a) *dc*   b) *ic*   c) *ls*   iii.   a) *dc*   b) *nm*   c) *nm*
   ii.   a) *nm*   b) *dc*   d) *nm*   iv.   a) *nm*   b) *dc*   d) *dc*

5.7   ⊔ Halls of Residence   ⌐ Nursing Block   ▭ Science Theatre   └ Library   ◯ Student Centre   ☐ Sports Centre
   Leaves library at 8.40. / Arrives at Economics Block at 8.45. / Arrives at Humanities Block A at 8.55. / Leaves Humanities Block B at 9.10. / Leaves School of Fashion and Textiles at 9.25. / Arrives at Sports Centre at 9.40.

5.8   a. the B group - nurses   b. anti-clockwise (opposite direction to Linda)   c. (they're) painting the (interior of the) Administration Building (this week)   d. after Linda's students have got their student cards

📄 READING ANSWERS 5.2 - 5.11 *(pages 82 - 86)*

5.2   1. Should employees be required to continue to study in order to keep their jobs?
   2. Do you think tertiary education should be free?

5.4   Paragraph 1. d   Paragraph 2. i   Paragraph 3. c   Paragraph 4. j   Paragraph 5. e
   Paragraph 6. a   Paragraph 7. g   Paragraph 8. f

5.5   Reason 1. b, m   Reason 2. h, l   Reason 3. k

5.6   1)   i.   f   ii.   d   iii.   b   iv.   a   v.   c   vi.   e
         2)   i.   f   ii.   e   iii.   d   iv.   a   v.   b   vi.   c
         3)   i.   a   ii.   f   iii.   d   iv.   c   v.   b   vi.   e

5.7   (1) educational   (2) individual   (3) paper   (4) stress   (5) part-time
         (6) overlooked   (7) undesirable   (8) applicants   (9) standards   (10) higher

5.8   (1) spend (vast amounts of) extra money   (2) to send their children to schools with a perceived edge
         (3) raise our intellectual standards / help improve the level of intelligence within the community
         (4) candidates with qualifications on paper   (5) studying after working hours
         (6) (the) extra workload (results in) abnormally high stress levels
         (7) alarmist   (8) Britain's education system (overall) is equal to (that of) any in the world

5.9   i. it is no secret   ii. hardly a new concept   iii. attitudinal changes

5.10   a. F   b. F   c. T   d. NG   e. T   f. NG   g. T   h. T

5.11   Dr. Gatsby's comments on university education were not well received.
        Critics point out that the rewards of study are usually far greater than the stress one experiences at the time.

✍ WRITING ANSWERS 5.1 - 5.4 *(pages 87 - 90)*

5.1   (1) six stages   (2) the first stage is   (3) second stage   (4) writing the first draft
         (5) a brief outline   (6) formal academic style   (7) stage number four   (8) writing a second draft
         (9) the final draft   (10) a spellcheck is required

5.2   The suggested arrangement of the paragraphs given in the model answer below is one of a number of suitable solutions to the problem:

MODEL ANSWER:

For this university course an essay is completed in six stages. The first stage is a private tutorial in which the task and topic are fully discussed with the tutor. A reading list should be obtained, detailing useful resource material.

The second stage involves conducting suitable research. Notes are taken from available literature at the library, and data collected from questionnaires, interviews and surveys. Writing the first draft is the third stage. First, it is necessary to organise the content of the essay and produce a brief outline. Next, the draft is written in the acceptable formal academic style and checked for appropriate language.

Stage number four is another tutorial or study group discussion, during which problem areas are analysed and further ideas and suggestions are noted. The fifth stage includes reading the resource material again before writing a second draft, using suggestions from stage four. Once completed, all quotations should be checked for errors.

The sixth stage consists of writing the final draft of the essay. A spellcheck is required before adding a title page and compiling a bibliography. The essay should then be submitted before the deadline for completion.

(192 words)

5.3   **MODEL ANSWER:**
&
5.4   Youth drug abuse is a serious problem nowadays in many cultures. Not only is illegal drug use on the rise, but children as young as 10 years old are experimenting with alcohol and tobacco. The reasons for this behaviour are unclear, but certain sociologists blame the examples set by their elders.

      Parents who drink and smoke to excess are, in effect, telling their children that it is acceptable to abuse their bodies with drugs. Consequently, children may have a similar view towards illegal drugs even if their parents are against their use. In addition, drug use shown on television and in films can only confuse children who are also taught at school that drug abuse is wrong.

      The pressure on young people to perform well at school in order to compete for jobs is a possible cause of the problem. Many believe they cannot live up to their parents' expectations and feel a sense of hopelessness. Also, the widespread availability of drugs means teenagers are faced with the temptation to experiment. Drugs are used as a means of expressing dissatisfaction with the pressures they face in society.

      The effects of drug abuse are well known. Many young people's talents are wasted and addiction to hard drugs can cost a user his or her life. Furthermore, those who drink and drive may be involved in fatal road accidents. The cost to society is great, and enormous amounts of money are spent on convicting drug dealers and on education programmes.

      To conclude, I recommend that the only sensible way to solve this problem is to educate young people about the dangers of drug use and to take steps to reduce the pressure of competition placed upon them.

(283 words)

?!   PUNCTUATION ANSWERS 5.1 - 5.2 *(page 92)*

5.1   (See Reading Passage 5 on page 83)

5.2   (See Listening Dictation 3 on page 109 of the Listening Tapescript)

❋   SPELLING ANSWERS 5.1 - 5.2 *(page 93)*

5.1   Young people are usually extremely critical of decisions made by persons in authority. This attitude is not always acceptable to the more powerful members of a society. They may feel threatened by the idealism of some university students; an idealism which often prevents the latter from viewing an issue **objectively**. Yet without student protests, certain injustices within society might never be exposed.

Although the community and the media usually **attack** student unrest at the time, many years later, as community **attitudes** change, the reasons for that student action become clearer, and generally their ideas, if not their methods, are considered more **acceptable**. If we can understand that it is probably in **society's** best interest for the young to question existing attitudes and injustices, we might realise that we would do well to listen more closely to what they have to say.

Perhaps older people should become more **tolerant of** the ideas and creative expression of the younger generation. Too often the ideas they express are dismissed simply **because** they are new. On the other hand, young people ought to recognise when they are being impossibly **selfish** and their demands are too impractical.

5.2

accommodation	(column 2)	appreciation	(column 1)	business	(column 3)
developing	(column 4)	entertainment	(column 3)	feasible	(column 1)
governmental	(column 2)	hypothetical	(column 1)	indefinite	(column 4)
indiscriminate	(column 4)	necessary	(column 1)	perspective	(column 4)
thorough	(column 2)	unsuccessful	(column 1)		

❋   GRAMMAR ANSWERS 5.1 - 5.7 *(pages 94 - 96)*

5.1
a.   C - of learning (the structure is 'the disadvantage(s) of *(doing)(something)* ')
b.   C - to develop (the structure is 'to enable *(someone)* to *(do)(something)* ')
c.   C - skills is ('the most problematical' is singular)
d.   A - Owing to ('due to' must be preceded by a noun or pronoun)
e.   C - On the other hand ('on the contrary' introduces the denial of a previously stated opposite)
f.   B - had to ('must' in the past is only possible with 'must have + past participle')
g.   C - be (modal verbs are followed by the infinitive)
h.   C - lacking (the structure is 'responsible for *(someone)((not) having)(something)* ')

5.2
a.   <u>Almost</u> the students think that <u>learning language</u> is hard because of the new <u>vocabularies</u>.
   → *Most of the students think that learning a language is hard because of the new vocabulary.*
b.   There are <u>another</u> reasons why <u>study</u> a language is difficult for <u>the oversea</u> students.
   → *There are other reasons (is another reason) why studying a language is difficult for overseas students.*
c.   I am very <u>exciting with</u> the chance to study <u>the</u> computer science in <u>the</u> foreign country.
   → *I am very excited about the chance to study computer science in a foreign country.*
d.   It is important to <u>practice your study</u> with different <u>nationality</u> classmate if it is possible.
   → *It is important to practise studying with classmates of different nationality if it is possible.*
e.   The chart <u>is giving many informations of</u> the number of <u>student</u> now <u>study</u> in Britain.
   → *The chart gives a lot of information about the number of students now studying in Australia.*
f.   The <u>educational</u> system in my country is not the same <u>with the other place</u>.

    → *The education system in my country is not the same as in other places.*

g. After <u>study</u>, I hope to <u>go travel over</u> the world and <u>enjoy to meet</u> new <u>peoples</u>.
    → *After studying, I hope to go travelling around the world, and I will enjoy meeting new people.*

5.3
i. the use of computers a few years ago / *whereas* (contrast) / the use of computers these days
ii. young people (their inquisitiveness and creativity) / *by comparison* (comparison) / older people (their inclination to experiment with new ideas)
iii. male students (the age at which they begin to develop an intellectual self-discipline) / *quite different to each other* (contrast) / female students (the age at which they begin to develop an intellectual self-discipline)
iv. sport (at a comprehensive school) / *likewise* (comparison) / sporting activities (at university)
v. youth today (their selfishness and unawareness of what is happening in the world) / *nowhere near as* (contrast) / what the media would have us believe (about youth today)
vi. European students' radicalism on campus / *while* (contrast) / Australian students' hard work to complete their studies.

5.5
1. Ayers Rock, Australia, is the biggest rock in the world.
2. The Amazon River is the longest river in the world.
3. Mont. Blanc is the highest mountain in Europe.
4. The United States is the world's most affluent nation.
5. China is the most populous/densely populated country on earth.
6. The diesel engine is the most economical vehicle engine.
7. Pluto is the least (well) understood planet in the solar system.
8. A score of 9 in IELTS is the best score that can be achieved. *(possible answer)*
9. Adolf Hitler was probably the worst dictator in modern history. *(possible answer)*
10. Albert Einstein was the most influential scientist of the twentieth century. *(possible answer)*

5.6   (1) a   (2) c   (3) a   (4) f   (5) b   (6) d   (7) g   (8) c   (9) c   (10) e   (11) b   (12) a

☆ VOCABULARY ANSWERS 5.1 *(page 97)*

5.1

Place	Person	Gerund/Thing	Adjective	Verb	Adverb
-	educator	educating/eduction	educated *	<u>educate</u>	-
teacher's college	teacher	<u>teaching</u>	taught *	teach	-
-	surveyor	surveying/survey	surveyed *	<u>survey</u>	-
-	instructor	instructing/instruction	<u>instructive</u>	instruct	instructively
study	student	<u>studying/study</u>	studious	study	studiously
-	-	ability	able	-	<u>ably</u>
practice	practitioner	<u>practising/practice</u>	practising/practised *	practise	-
performance hall	<u>performer</u>	performing/performance	performing/performed *	perform	-
-	assessor	assessing/assessment	assessed *	<u>assess</u>	-
-	qualifier	qualifying/qualification	qualifying/qualified *	qualify	-
academy	academic	academia	academic	-	academically

NB: The given words in the exercise are underlined.

* past participles (and '-ing' forms) may also be adjectival in some cases i.e. *an educated person* (taught / surveyed / practised / performed / assessed / qualified)

✿ IELTS QUIZ ANSWERS 5.1 - 5.5 *(pages 98 - 99)*

5.1   a. 2 hours 45 minutes   b. within two weeks   c. once only   d. three passages
e. in Writing Task 2 (both Academic and General Training Modules); in Writing Task 1 (General Training Module) - when you have to write a letter.   f. 3 parts   g. Part 2   h. Reading and Listening only
i. three months

5.2   1. a   2. b   3. c

5.3   a. F   b. T   c. F   d. F   e. T   f. T   g. F

5.4   a. plan the number of paragraphs to write   b. in the Academic Module, no; but in the General Training Module, if you are asked to write a letter, you should follow the usual letter writing conventions which include a final conclusive paragraph.   c. the topic / the topic question.
d. refutation paragraph

5.5   should do: a.   d.   e.

       should not do: b.   c.   f.   g.   h.   i.

30 PRACTICE FOR MULTIPLE CHOICE QUESTIONS

The given multiple choice answers are either **directly or indirectly supported** (correct), **directly or indirectly contradicted** (incorrect), or **not mentioned** at all (incorrect).

Examine the 3 (or more) possible answers to see how multiple choice tasks are constructed. Since there is usually only one correct answer - the instructions tell you if more than one answer is possible (see also Hint 31) - it follows that the other answers must either be **definitely wrong** (contradicted in the passage) or **not mentioned** at all.

First, look at the ways in which answer choices may be incorrect:

1. There is often at least one given answer choice that is **neither sensible nor logical**.

2. There may be given answer choices that are **contradicted** in the passage.

   A choice may either be

	directly contradicted	- clearly and directly opposite in meaning to what is heard
or	**indirectly contradicted**	- what is heard leads you to conclude that the choice is incorrect
or	**not exactly what is stated**	- almost, but not quite, what the speaker says.

3. There may be given answer choices that are **not mentioned** in the passage. (Note that some answers might not be mentioned in the passage and may also lack logic or sense.)

Next, look at the ways in which answer choices may be correct:

1. A given answer choice may be **directly supported** by what is stated in the passage.

2. A given answer choice may be **indirectly supported** by what is stated in the passage, that is, what is heard leads you to conclude that the choice is the correct answer.

When you practise, ask yourself if the given answer choices in a multiple choice question are:

- directly supported .... *ds*		- directly contradicted .... *dc*	
- indirectly supported .... *is*		- indirectly contradicted .... *ic*	
- not **exactly** what is stated .... *ne*		- lacking logic or sense .... *ls*	
- not mentioned .... *nm*		- "all or none of the above" .... *a or n*	

31 MULTIPLE CHOICE - CONSIDER ALL OF THE CHOICES

Consider **all** of the possible answer choices. The **last choice** may be one of the following two types:

   1. **"all of the above"** answer choices are correct   or   2. **"none of the above"** is correct.

If you do not read the last choice given, and it asks you to consider **all** of the other choices as correct or incorrect answers, you might easily make a choice that only **partly** answers the question.

49 LOOK FOR PATTERNS OF WORDS AND PHRASES

Finding the answers to questions in the Reading Test depends on your ability to recognise **the shapes and patterns in groups of words**. There are basically 3 kinds of "patterns" in groups of words to recognise:

Pattern Type 1	... with **exactly the same pattern**	i.e. with exactly the same words
Pattern Type 2	... with **a similar pattern**	i.e. with one (or more) words substituted
Pattern Type 3	... with **a less recognisable pattern**	i.e. with different words but the same or similar meaning to the words sought

Question: Permanent damage to the body may result if Ecstasy is taken simultaneously with ... (?)

		Question Phrase		**Passage Phrase**
(Pattern Type 1)	...	'may result'	→	'may result'
(Pattern Type 2)	...	'taken simultaneously'	→	'taken at the same time'
(Pattern Type 3)	...	'damage to the body	→	'harm to bodily organs'

59   PAY ATTENTION TO THE PRESENTATION

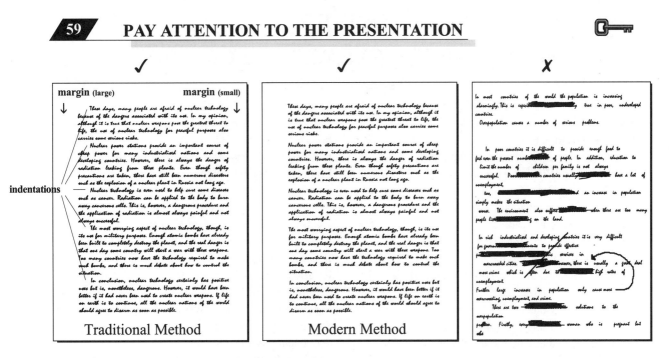

While it is true that the IELTS Writing Test is not marked for neatness, you should still consider the psychological aspect of the task when you are trying to impress an examiner. You are not there in person to present your work, so always aim to make your writing look presentable on the page.

10 Point Guide to Presentation and Layout

i. There is no need for a title in the IELTS test task writings, and do not rewrite the question task.

ii. Use left and right margins as in the two good examples above.

iii. Use either **indentations** for the first line of each paragraph (traditional method) or a **blank line** between paragraphs (modern method), but do not mix both methods.

iv. Do not use double spacing, that is, do not leave a blank line between each line of writing.

v. Use all the line - write from the very edge of the left margin all the way to the very edge of the right margin. This is true for every line, except where the line is short, or where the last word will not fit between the margins. In the latter case, do not continue into the margin area. Start on a new line with the word that is too large.

vi. Do not split words. Rather than memorise complex rules for splitting words, do not split them.

vii. Write between 10-12 words per line. This will prevent you writing words too large and with gaps larger than a single letter or two between words. It will also make it simpler for you to quickly estimate how many words you have written in the test.

viii. *Use cursive writing, that is, with the letters joined together.*

Cursive writing makes your work look more mature, if it can be read easily. The non-cursive writing of some candidates can look immature. Since first impressions are important, impress the examiner by writing the way educated English-speaking adults usually write in English.

ix. Write in a thick, not fine, pen, and consider writing in blue ink. Why? From a psychological point of view, a thick pen makes a stronger impression. Similarly, written work in pencil looks weak and impermanent. Pencil users waste time erasing, and sharpening or pumping the lead. Blue ink is more soothing and pleasant to look at than black. Leave behind a positive impression.

x. If you make a mistake, simply cross out the ~~error~~ error with one line. There is no penalty for crossing out. Besides, it shows the examiner that you are capable of error correction.

(Adapted from *'101 Helpful Hints for IELTS'*)

INDEX
to '202 USEFUL EXERCISES FOR IELTS'